Christian Understanding of the Beginnings, the Process and the Outcome of World History

CHRISTIAN UNDERSTANDING OF THE BEGINNINGS, THE PROCESS AND THE OUTCOME OF WORLD HISTORY

Via Universalis

Paul C. Merkley

Toronto Studies in Theology
Volume 83

The Edwin Mellen Press

BR
115
.H5
M33
2001

Library of Congress Cataloging-in-Publication Data

Merkley, Paul Charles.
  Christian understanding of the beginning, the process and the outcome of world history
: via universalis / Paul C. Merkley.
      p. cm. -- (Toronto studies in theology ; v. 83)
  Includes bibliographical references and index.
  ISBN 0-7734-7512-5
  1. History (Theology) I. Title. II. Series.

  BR115.H5 M33   2001
  231.7'6--dc21

                                                                00-048728

This is volume 83 in the continuing series
Toronto Studies in Theology
Volume 83 ISBN 0-7734-7512-5
TST Series ISBN 0-88946-975-X

A CIP catalog record for this book is available from the British Library.

          The Edwin Mellen Press   The Edwin Mellen Press
                 Box 450   Box 67
          Lewiston, New York   Queenston, Ontario
          USA 14092-0450   CANADA L0S 1L0

                        The Edwin Mellen Press, Ltd.
                        Lampeter, Ceredigion, Wales
                        UNITED KINGDOM SA48 8LT

                     Printed in the United States of America

Dedication

... AS ALWAYS, TO GWEN.

Christian Understanding of the Beginnings, the Process, and Outcome of World History: Via Universalis

CONTENTS

Preface

Paul Merkley's book, *Christian Understanding of the Beginnings, the Process and the Outcome of World History: Via Universalis* should find many appreciative readers among Theologians, Biblical Scholars and Philosophers. It is rare to find a professional historian who is willing and able to engage in the task of theological integration. A senior historian at a prestigious Canadian University, Professor Merkley is one of very few persons qualified to engage in this important project of integration. The project itself is almost breath-taking in its daring: to offer interpretation of history that discloses its universal meaning. Such universal interpretations of history were once an accepted genre, but since the Enlightenment they have atrophied to the point of extinction. And yet the Judaeo-Christian faith, as a historical religion, does claim that the unfolding story of humanity is not a meaningless chaos of events plunging haphazardly this way and that and ending in oblivion but rather lies under the sovereign providence of God and is therefore a teleological process imbued with significance. Professor Merkley dares as a historian to take seriously this teleological claim and seeks to discern within the advance of world history a pattern culminating in God's eschatological purpose. The originality and boldness of this proposal, from an eminent historian should not be underestimated.

William Lane Craig, Ph.D., D.Theol.
Talbot School of Theology.

Chapter One : "This Is The Universal Way."

The faithful Abraham received this divine message ... : "In your seed all nations will be blessed" [*Gen.* 22:18]. Now Abraham was by birth a Chaldean, but he was bidden to leave his country, his family, and his father's house, so that he might receive this promise, and that from him might issue the "seed prepared for by the ministry of angels, the mediator offering his hand" [*Galatians* 3:19]; so that in this mediator should be found that universal way for the soul's liberation, the way made available for all nations ... Hence, so long afterwards, the Saviour, who took flesh from "the seed of Abraham", said of himself, "I am the way, the truth and the life" [*John* 14:6] ... This means that the way does not belong to one people, but it is for all nations; and the Law and the Word of God did not stay in Sion and Jerusalem but went out from there so that it might spread through the whole world.
- Augustine of Hippo, *The City of God*, Book X, Chapter 32. [1]

....

World History

(i) Textbook Considerations.

Of the generation that produced the baby-boom, only a small minority went to college; consequently, the market for textbooks on World Civilization or World History was much smaller then than it is today. In those days, the college History textbooks (Ferguson and Bruun, H.A.L. Fisher, Palmer and Coulton), were informed by a positive, sometimes even buoyant, spirit. The world is about to enter an era marked by the gobalizing of the blessings of Modern Life; the United States, having recently become the principal defender of Western civilization, is leading the Western world in the task of distributing the values of democracy and social equality, along with the blessings of prosperity, throughout the world. The very layout of the Page of Contents reflects a worldview now long gone. The textbook authors lead the readers immediately onto the path of description of the origins of the earliest civilizations (in the Tigris-Euphrates valleys and in the Nile Valley), and proceed to tell the Story So Far along a pathway paved with the consequences following from the deeds of those who led those ancient kingdoms.

The place of History has been drastically reduced in the college curriculum today. Still, given the multiplication of enrolment at colleges and universities since the baby-boomers came of age, the English-language college market in World Civilization or World History texts is huge and lucrative, although dominated by a surprisingly small number of texts - which circumstance makes the task of generalizing about their contents and their spirit manageable. The spirit which informs the current textbooks is entirely different from that which informed the earlier ones. Along the way, the buoyant spirit has given way to a spirit of apology for the sins of the Western past. The transition to this anti-European, "non-linear" worldview began slowly in the early Sixties, but accelerated in the "Vietnam years," when college audiences demanded, and faculty gleefully provided, a new style of denigration of the received culture ("The System.")

A striking characteristic of today's introductory college textbooks in World History is that all begin with determined statements of their intention to cast aside the European-centredness that has hitherto blighted the mind of the English-language reader of the book. It is simply assumed that the reader is aware of this blight on his mind and character, and is as fed up with it as is the author. It is assumed, further, that the reader will agree that this is something that conventional learning or The System has done to him, that he welcomes the radical alternative implied by what is being proposed to him, and is eager to participate in the liberating consequences. Here we have an instance of the governing paradox in University undergraduate learning: that the ascendant cliches of secular humanism must always be presented as pioneer discoveries - bold new truths that will allow the undergraduate exit from convention and entry into the freemasonry of enlightened minds.

But the most astonishing aspect of all of this is that the textbook writers never deliver upon their promises. After the heady talk of the first few pages - after the section on Origins of Life, The Geological Record, The Cradle of Humanity ("Early Man"), and Distribution of Primitive Agricultural Societies (typically about ten to 15 pages in all, out of perhaps 800 to 1000 pages) - all the exciting promise of restructuring The Story of Mankind on universal or global lines is simply forgotten.

There is a simple reason for this. "The Story of Mankind" cannot be told "globally." It cannot begin and continue with accumulating meanings, until the author has chosen *where* to begin. And it follows as the night the day that to choose is also to reject. This is the fundamental logic that the authors of

World History textbooks simply will not address.

*   *   *

In his "Preface" to *The World Since 1500: A Global History*, L.S. Stavrianos invites "you, the reader [to see what follows as though you were] perched upon the moon" - in other textbooks, it is Mars! - "looking down on our whole vast planet ...":

> This global approach is a departure from traditional modern history ... We cannot truly understand either Western or non-Western history unless we have our "lunar" global overview that encompasses both. Then we can see how much interaction there has been between all peoples in all times, and how important that interaction has been in determining the course of human history.
>
> At first the interaction was fitful and rather slight. But then Columbus and da Gama set forth on their overseas exploration ... Within a few decades they and their successors brought all parts of the world into direct contact, and the intimacy of that contact has grown steadily to the present day. By contrast, the various human communities prior to 1500 had existed in varying degrees of isolation .... [T]he role of Western Europe in this early modern period is emphasized, not because of any Western orientation, but because from a global viewpoint Europe at this time was in fact the dynamic source of global change ... Finally, in the twentieth century, world history becomes the story of the growing reaction against Western domination, and the dangerous groping toward a new world balance. [2]

Notice how the author tacks confusedly between two antagonistic premises: (a) that World History can be told as a linear story because it is centered in the adventures ("dynamic") of the one set of actors, beginning with Columbus, who brought the previously discrete civilizations into their present common destiny; and (b), that World History can be told as a linear story because, provided our angle of vision is "lunar," "we can see how much interaction there has been between all peoples in all times." "The precise degree of this interaction," he concedes a few lines further, "varied enormously according to time and location." This is an evasion of the first order, as appears immediately when we get into the main text of the book. In the first lines of Chapter One ("Introduction: From Regional to Global History") we read:

> Why should a history begin with the year 1500? ... The answer is that until 1500 humans had lived largely in regional isolation. The various racial groups had been scattered about in a pattern of virtual global segregation ... Indeed, world history in the strict sense did not begin until the voyages of Columbus and da Gama and Magellan. Prior to their exploits, there were relatively parallel histories of separate peoples rather than one unified history of humankind. During the long millennia of the Paleolithic period, Homo sapiens gradually scattered from their birthplace in Africa to all the continents except Antarctica. Then the ending of the Ice Age raised the level of the oceans, thereby splitting Africa from Europe, the Americas from Northeast Asia, and Australia from Southeast Asia, to mention only the major separations ... It is Eurasia that constitutes the "heartland" of world history. It is the place of origin of the earliest and most advanced civilizations of mankind. Prior to 1500, world history was essentially of Eurasia, as here defined. [3]

Stavrianos' logic, in making the process of European penetration into all the other civilizations of the globe the informing theme of World History since 1500, is absolutely unexceptionable. But the corollaries that follow from this premise Stavrianos simply refuses to notice. One is that the informing theme of World History *prior* to this point (1500) must be the Story So Far: that is, the story of the origins and development of the Civilization which played this role: *that* story (as Stavrianos' concedes in passing) is the only history that we can trace to the origins of Civilization itself ("... it is the place of origin of the earliest and most advanced civilizations of mankind.") In total contradiction of this strongly stated premise, but in a moment of ritual genuflection to the anthropological (that is, the anti-historical) model preferred by other textbook writers, Stavrianos then teases us with the possibility of tracing the Story So Far from the "birthplace in Africa" (about which, more in Chapter Two.) But Stavrianos has already dammed up that path to the present when he conceded (mildly, considering the historical realities) the essential fact of "regional isolation" of human communities prior to 1500.

The circumstance that Stavrianos is only required to tell the story from 1500 forward would, one would have thought, have excused him from these gestures to anthropology and our "hominid ancestors." One suspects that what dictates this gesture is the author's sense that, to be taken seriously, he must be clearly seen to be cutting the cord of connection between his story (The World Since 1500) and the traditional Judaeo-Christian account of World History, which is the only account that allows us to take the story back to a documentable point of origin, and then to tell it forward as a continuous story with accumulating meaning. But this Judaeo-Christian account of World History is all bound up with theological claims; and the secular textbook author must be seen to be washing his hands of these. Hence the gesture to anthropology and the evolutionary world-view.

All the World History textbooks nowadays begin with the ritual exorcism of "European chauvinism." The latest edition of the widely-used textbook by Wallbank *et al.*, begins:

> Originally published in 1942, *Civilization Past & Present* was the first text of its kind. Its objective was to present a survey of world cultural history, treating the development and growth of civilization not as a unique European experience but as a global one through which all the great culture systems have interacted to produce the present-day world ... [W]e are of the same species, and we share a fundamental communality that connects present with past: the human environmental nexus. It is the dynamic interplay of environmental factors and human activities that accounts for the terrestrial process known as history . [4]

The *Columbia History of the World*, by Garraty and Gay, stresses the same theme:

> We live in the Age of World History, and as ages go, ours is relatively young. Until the fifteenth century, the many cultures of this earth developed in comparative isolation, their boundaries breached only by occasional traders, by border warfare, and by spectacular mass migrations, such as the "barbarian" invasion of the Roman Empire in the early centuries of the Christian Era. But after Columbus and Cortes had awakened the people of Western Europe to the possibilities, their appetites for converts, profits, and fame was thoroughly aroused and Western civilization was introduced, mainly by force, over nearly all the globe ... The people of these continents [Africa, Asia, and the Americas] were, in short, the victims of a ruthless unrelenting exploitation ... World history is hard to write, but this has not discouraged historians from writing it ever since the beginning of the craft among the ancient Greeks [*sic!*]

Then, almost immediately, and (one assumes inadvertently) contradicting the falsehood about Greek invention of history:

> History begins in the Near East. As we have seen, the cradle of humanity lies probably elsewhere, but the historian's narrative cannot begin at the creation of the first Adam [*sic!*]. The slow biological emergence of Homo sapiens, the sort of human being we are, precedes history, and the greater part of the existence of Homo sapiens also ran before the beginning of history .... All of the oldest homonid fossils ... come from southern and eastern Africa. The oldest of them, from the Omo River in Ethiopia, are nearly four million years old .... But a continuous persisting society was late in coming. It came into being first in the Near East, and thus the historical tradition of Babylon and Egypt became the fountainhead of our historical memory .[5]

In the textbook by Stanley Chodorow. *et. ai.,* we read: "The earliest discernible stage in the development of culture was common to human communities wherever they existed. Only later did geographical and political isolation produce the characteristics of distinctive cultures. The first chapters of the book are, therefore, worldwide in vision and approach " [6] - which means, of course, that the first chapters of the text are Darwinian anthropology, and not history at all.

Survey of all the rival textbooks reveals these recurring features:

(A) The immediate and unqualified condemnation of our historiographical tradition for putting Western Civilization at the centre of the story. This is usually accompanied by explicit reproach of our own dark past, (its "ruthless, unrelenting exploitation," in the Garraty/Gay text). This is then followed immediately by,

(B) The announcement of a bold departure from this tradition by means of a pioneer kind of "objective" (lunar or Martian) and/or "comparative" approach. (The claim to pioneer standing for the text and its authors is always made, notwithstanding the fact that it has been conventional now already for a generation or more for textbooks to trumpet this approach ! This allows the readers to feel themselves part of a bold campaign of renunciation of the conventional tyrannies.) Then,

(C) A statement on the long history of "interaction" among all the "civilizations" (or "cultures" - the words are not always distinguished) - carefully qualified or expressed ambiguously.

At this point, the textbook writers divide into two sub-types. The more cautious choose this point to make the painful admission

(D): that the *historical record* begins *somewhere in particular* (namely, the Near East), and that apart from this historical record there is only guesswork about the huge blocks of time and space presumably implied in generalization C.

The less responsible, however, proceed immediately from C to

(E): Declaration of a new beginning for the telling of the whole Story of Mankind where there is no written record (and therefore no history) - in the prehistoric fossil record. From this point forward, environmental determinism explains the variety of cultures and civilizations.

Stavrianos and the *Columbia History* are examples of texts that include step D. Wallbank and Chodorow are examples of the texts that proceed immediately from C to E. A particularly blatant example of the latter sub-type (and one with which I close this survey) is this by John P. McKay, et. al.:

> Chapter One: New Eastern Origins
> The culture of the modern Western world has its origins in places as far away as modern Iraq, Iran and Egypt. In these areas human beings abandoned their life of roaming and hunting to settle in stable agricultural communities. From these communities grew cities and civilizations, societies that invented concepts and techniques that have become integral parts of contemporary life. Fundamental is the development of writing by the Sumerians in Mesopotamia, an invention that enables knowledge of the past to be preserved and facilitates the spread and accumulating of learning, lore, literature, and science. Mathematics, astronomy, and architecture were all innovations of the ancient Near Eastern civilizations. So too were the first law codes and religious concepts that still permeate daily life.
> How did wild hunters become urban dwellers? How did the roots of Western culture establish themselves in far-off Mesopotamia [What is Mesopotamia "far- off" from?] and what caused Mesopotamian culture to become predominant throughout most of the ancient Near East? What part did the Egyptians play in this vast story? Lastly, what did the arrival of the Hittites on the fringes of Mesopotamia and Egypt mean to the superior cultures of their new neighbors? These are the questions this chapter will explore.
> On December 17, 1831, young Charles Darwin stepped aboard the H.M.S. Beagle to begin a voyage to South America and the Pacific Ocean ...

Just like that! The key to all the mysteries! Then follow eight sentences summarizing Darwin's theories. And then the conclusion: "The theories of Darwin, supported by the evidence of fossilized remains, ushered in a new scientific era, an era in which scientists and scholars have re-examined the very nature of human beings and their history." [7]

There are World Civilization textbooks which apologize for the "European bias" of their content, but nonetheless lay out the story on the old lines. And there are World Civilization textbooks (like that by McKay, just cited) that tantalize the reader with the prospect of a radical restructuring of the story beginning somewhere else or nowhere else. None of them ever actually does this, however. The reason is simply that it cannot be done. Nonetheless, the ruinous impression is implanted: that it is merely conventional that we organize the story of World History around the B.C./A.D. axis. Despite all the solemn scientific mummery, these assaults on "convention" have nothing whatever to do with allegiance to objective fact or inductive method, and everything to do with the contemporary intellectual's temperamental and ideological commitment to denigration of our civilization's origins in Judaism.

(ii) The Traditional Understanding of World History.

There are some truths that are exceptionally difficult to defend, precisely because they are axiomatic. Such is the case with what we propose in this chapter.

World History is not the only method for recital of the past; it is, however, the only method which is capable of telling the whole story of the human past as a single narrative, having a single direction and accumulating meanings, occurring entirely on the ground of human time.

Outsiders to the Christian faith reject the theological propositions which make possible confidence in the unity and the purposefulness of history. They should understand, however, that there is no possibility of embracing the latter (the unity and purposefulness of history) without embracing the former (Christian theology).

Outsiders to our civilization - nations and tribes and clans and communities of all sorts - maintain their various traditional recitals of the parts of the past that belong to them. But however spiritually satisfying these (to us) esoteric modes of recital may be to those who belong to the cultures which formed them, they break down completely when it comes to the challenge of incorporating all the diverse accounts of all *other* peoples. It is not possible, for example, to incorporate the stories of all the peoples of the world into Inuit legends, and tell the whole as a consecutive, linear narrative, with accumulating meanings, entirely occurring on the ground of human time.

"World History" is the *universal* mode of recital of the past, in precisely the same sense and for precisely the same reasons that the Christian calendar is the universally governing calendar. The universal hegemony of the Christian calendar is the practical face of the universal hegemony of World History - the universal mode of recital of the past. Even if there were no one, anywhere, at this moment reflecting on the meanings behind the Christian claims, it would still be true that we are all at this moment carrying out our commitments to each other by reckoning forward from that one fixed moment in time, which recalls the birth of the Saviour, and which was given this function because our ancestors were convinced that everything takes its relative importance from its position *vis--a-vis* that moment. In precisely the same sense, the various political communities in the world must relate their political claims to each other in terms of the singular catalogue of political meanings that is supposed to follow from the one method of narrating the whole story of mankind as a single story with a single direction. This is the narrative we call World History, whose entire content is organized (speaking only practically now) upon this same allegedly pivotal event.

World History has achieved its standing as the universal method of recital of the whole story of the past because it alone has the resources for bringing all the diverse and far-flung stories of the past into one account. At this moment, Arab nations and Israel are clamouring for respect for their different definitions of their "rights" before the United Nations and before the Great Powers; in doing so, both sides put forth interpretations of the same catalogue of treaties and historical occasions. For a need, their spokesmen are prepared to go back to the U.N. Resolution 181 for the Partition of Palestine (November 29, 1947), then back behind that to the Balfour Declaration (November 2, 1917), to the Congress of Berlin (1878), to decisions of the Ottomon Sultans, to Suleiman the Magnificent, to the Crusaders, to the Roman Emperors, to Alexander, to Hammurabi, and if you press them hard enough to Jacob and Esau, Isaac and Ishamael, and to Abraham. North American aboriginal peoples will not take you back so far; but they will take you back a shorter distance along that very same single linear account, World History, which describes how one great global-political state-of-affairs gave way to another. There is only one such account, and all political claims must be addressed on its ground, and not some other ground.

There are reasons for this. It is not possible to tell the whole story of mankind as a single story having a single direction and accumulating meanings, occurring entirely on the ground of human time, unless everyone agrees to found its latest chapters on The Story So Far. It was European Civilization, not Chinese, Indian, African or any other Civilization, which in a moment of time (the end of the Fifteenth Century and the early Sixteenth) went out into the world and began the work of drawing all the other civilizations of the world into acquaintance with itself and with each other, establishing (on its own terms, for the most part) the distribution of political, social, economic and cultural privileges that would obtain among the human communities. This is the story of European Empire. Questions of right and wrong, fairness or unfairness, are utterly irrelevant to our present theme. We are speaking practically.

The key to understanding any single issue in political, cultural, or economic reality in any corner of the world today is that it is one of the outcomes of this process of the globalizing of human destiny which was inaugurated in the era of European Empire, beginning roughly in the mid-Fifteenth Century, A.D.. Since it was European and not any other Civilization that played and plays this role, there is only one path that leads us back from the present moment of conflict to the *meaning* of the conflict. It is the story of the adventures of European civilization which contains the meanings that explain the dynamics of this process of globalizing of human destiny.

It is not true that the mode of recital of the past which our civilization developed simply elbowed its way brutishly into the lives of all the various peoples of the world, toppling their entirely adequate schemes of historical meaning, and clearing the debris to rear ours on the same ground. There is not now and there never has been any other adequate method for telling the whole story of mankind as a single, linear narrative, having accumulating meanings, and entirely occurring upon the ground of human time.

*   *   *

Chapter Two : The Legacy of Abram.

"The LORD said to Abram ..."

Stephen, the first known martyr of the Christian faith, is described early in the Book of Acts of the Apostles, standing before the council of the priests of Jerusalem. Witnesses against him charged that,

> "This man never ceases to speak words again this holy place and the law; for we heard him say that this Jesus of Nazareth will destroy this place, and will change the customs which Moses delivered to us."
> And gazing at him, all who sat in the council saw that his face was like the face of an angel.
> And the high priest said, "Is this so?
> And Stephen said:
> "Brethren and fathers, hear me. The God of glory appeared to our father Abraham, when he was in Mesopotamia, before he lived in Haran, and said to him, 'Depart from your land and from your kindred, and go into the land which I will show you.' Then he departed from the land of the Chaldeans, and lived in Haran ... " (*Acts* 6:13a, 7:4a).

Then follows Stephen's condensed version of God's dealing with Abraham and Abraham's descendants, leaving off with mention of Solomon and the building of the First Temple - leaving off, not voluntarily, it appears, but because his summary forecast of what follows ("You stiff-necked people, uncircumcised in heart and ears, you always resist the Holy Spirit. As your fathers did, so do you. Which of the prophets did not your fathers persecute?" [7:51-52a]) - enraged his listeners; and so they seized him, and put him to death (7:54-8:1).

Elsewhere throughout the New Testament as well, we see that the people of the primitive Church understood themselves to be the heirs to and the outcome of Abraham's initial response to God's address to him. They saw the whole story of mankind to this point as the ramification of that singular decision, made in a singular moment of time. They expected all that remains of the human story to be controlled, from this moment until its consummation, by the consequences of their decision, in faith. [1]

And so we follow Stephen's lead and return to the calling of Abraham, for instruction in the elements of Theory of History.

*   *   *

In *Genesis* 12:1-4, we read:

> Now the LORD said to Abram, "Go from your country and your kindred and your father's house to the land that I will show you. And I will make of you a great nation, and I will bless you, and make your name great, so that you will be a blessing. I will bless those who bless you, and him who curses you I will curse; and by you all the families of the earth will bless themselves."

Since modern scientific archeology began its work in the Middle East about a century and a half ago, hoardes of discovered artifacts and documents have shed ever-increasing light on the world into which Abram was born. [2] We now have "a remarkably detailed picture of life in ancient Mesopotamia, particularly as it affected the origins of the Hebrew peoples." [3] From these we learn, for example, that "Abram" was in fact a common West Semitic personal name. Whatever dignified associations belonged to this personal name ("High Father"? "Father of Aram"?, etc.) apparently there was no short supply of ordinary people who carried the name and its associations with them. Later, (*Genesis* 17) God will change Abram's name to Abraham ("Father of Nations.") [4] Likewise, the name of Ur, the city from which Abraham's father took his family "to go onto the land of Canaan" (*Gen.* 11:31) now turns out to have been a common name, possibly even a generic name for cities in ancient Mesopotamia.[5] Haran, the city where Abraham's father settled, where Abraham was living when "the LORD said to him, 'Go from your country and your kindred and father's house,' has the meaning "highway", or "crossroads" (as appears, again, from comparison with items from these rich archeological finds.) Abraham is called out at the crossroads of his life - but equally (that is, consequently, if we follow Stephen), at the "crossroads" of all lives since.

Called out from what?

Genesis makes clear that civilization, as our textbooks define it, had been in place for many generations when God's call came to Abraham, and indeed that Abraham's family had lived in civilized society for many generations. The longer the archeologists work at the setting of this story (today's Iraq and Syria) the clearer it becomes that Abraham was leaving a civilization whose longevity measures not in centuries merely but in millennia:

> To us who live in this late day, the second millennium [in the early third of which Abraham's lifetime probably falls] seems very long ago indeed. We are tempted to think of it as lying near the dawn of time, when man first struggled up from savagery into the light of history, and are prone, therefore, to underestimate its cultural achievements. We are further prone to picture the Hebrew ancestors, tent-dwelling wanderers that they were, as the most primitive of nomads, cut off by their mode of life from contact with what

culture there was, whose religion was the crudest sort of animism or polydaemonism ... This, however, is an erroneous notion and a symptom of want of perspective - a carry-over from the days when little was known at first hand of the ancient Orient ... The earliest decipherable inscriptions both in Egypt and in Mesopotamia reach back to the early centuries of the third millennium B.C. - thus approximately a thousand years before Moses. There [i.e., c. 2800- 2500, with the appearance of decipherable inscriptions,] history, properly speaking, begins. Moreover, in the course of the last few decades discoveries in all parts of the Bible world, and beyond it, have revealed a succession of yet earlier cultures which reach back through the fourth millennium, and fifth, and the sixth, to the seventh and, in some instances, further still. The Hebrews were in fact late comers on history's stage. All across the Bible lands, cultures had come to birth, assumed classical form, and run their course for hundreds and even thousands of years before Abraham was born. Difficult as it is for us to realize, it is actually further in time from the beginnings of civilization in the Near East to the age of Israel's origins than it is from that latter age to our own. [6]

The Bible's account of Abraham and his descendants takes for granted the long accomplishments of civilization, but shows little interest in accounting for them. *Civilization is not the goal of the story which the Bible begins to tell with this decision of Abraham.* Civilization is a reality already in place, part of the background of the story which begins here and which hereafter carries the meaning and the purpose of history. For the Bible, the story of civilization is pre-History. *History begins as the story of God's dealings with a limited number of individuals whom He has chosen in order to accomplish, by stages which will ultimately encompass the whole human community, the redemption of the human and the natural order.* As readers of this text, we are promised *explicitly* (12:2-3) that tracing the consequences of this story will lead us to history's outcome.

The Book of *Genesis* does not forbid our interest in questions of the origin and character and the meaning of civilization, but itself offers little towards answering such questions.   The story it has to tell is the story of redemption. This is not just the "theme", it is the *content* of its story. This (if we are faithful to its vision) is the whole of World History.

Genesis takes it for granted, as something   universally perceived by sensitive souls, that nature is at odds with us: that while we cannot realize anything in this life except through nature, that nonetheless it finally frustrates our inborn desire for tranquility and security; that it inflicts pain on us, and unfailingly lets us down, betrays us, turns against us, in the death of our bodies. *Genesis* offers understanding of this mystery (the ambiguous relationship of the individual soul to nature) in its stories of the Creation, the temptation of Eve and Adam, the banishment from Eden   (the original, perfect natural setting), the murder of Abel by Cain, the Flood, and the renewal of human society   in   a new,   more limited and less genial setting (signified by   the permission to live by eating the flesh of animals).   This does not amount to much as information about how and when and by what means these fundamental things happened.   What is given is far more valuable: profoundly disturbing, but then ultimately reassuring, insights into the *moral   meaning* of our ambiguous standing vis-a-vis nature.

In exactly the same spirit, *Genesis* takes it for granted, as something universally perceived by sensitive souls, that *civilization* is at odds with us. All the people with whom *Genesis* deals live in civilized settings. They need the tools of civilization - the gift of *writing*, for instance, for the preservation of this story. Nonetheless, civilization cannot satisfy our greatest need, which is the need   for self-realization. The Nineteen Century idealist philosopher Immanuel Kant expressed this mystery in non-theological terms: "Man wants concord ... but nature knows better what is good for his kind; nature wants discord." Kant saw civilization as the sum of all the ways we have of organizing the sum of all the individual strivings for "happiness". "To be happy," he admitted, "is necessarily the desire of every rational but finite being ... [but] it lies in the nature of human desires that they can never be wholly satisfied ... The infinitely manifold and unstable world of happiness, in itself without foundation or ultimate aim, is the medium of a realization which is subject to other conditions and other guidance." [7]

Genesis offers us some understanding of this mystery (the ambiguous relationship between the individual soul and civilization) in the form of several episodes in the long drama of transition from the earliest to the latest stages of the growth of human society. The story of Cain and Abel (Chapter 4) reflects, at least incidentally, on the tragic story of warfare between agricultural and grazing cultures, a feature of the earliest chapters in the organization of human society. Cain, the farmer, is himself banished from the soil; he becomes a wanderer, and his offspring establish the cities and found the arts and the industries (4:16-22). Civilization begins with the stigma of its founders' descent from the first murderer. Of Noah's three sons, who collectively are responsible for rebuilding human community after the Flood, it is Ham who sets us back on the old path of failure and disgrace (9:20-27), and it is Ham's son, Nimrod, who is the founder of the first great empire (*Gn* 18:8-10; cf. *I Chr* 1:10). Ever afterward, political empire carries the stigma of this criminal descent. [8]

As we can see, the Book of *Genesis* does not celebrate civilization. It is not, however, from the standpoint of mysticism or quietism that it judges civilization. It is not because civilization draws us from tranquility and contentment that it thwarts us. On the contrary, the first commandment (of the 613 commandments that Orthodox Judaism finds in the Bible) is "Be fruitful and multiply, and fill the earth and subdue it ..." (*Gen.* 1:28). The story of the Tower of Babel makes clear that the goal of our singular and collective life is not tranquility. Rabbi Gunther Plaut, summarizing the traditional reading of this story, writes:

> The sin of the generation of Babel consisted in their refusal to "fill
> the earth" ... [The sin of the generation of Babel is therefore not so
> much] arrogance but anxiety ... Babel was the city, and, to the anti-
> urban tradition of the Bible, its downfall appeared as a proper divine
> judgement. Babel referred of course to Babylon, but it also
> symbolized all empire building, corruption, arrogance, craving to
> erect monuments, desire for fame; it meant a turning away from what
> were considered the primary occupations of man - agriculture and
> the tending of flocks. Farmers and nomads "fill the earth," i.e.,
> they live close to it and its creatures; city-dwellers flee from the
> earth. Babel was an alienation of man from the simple life, and it is
> no accident that the Bible next turns to Abraham, a semi-nomad, as
> the source of all future blessings. [9]

The Book of *Genesis* offers a meager amount of anything that could be
called "information" about the origins of civilization, but an inexhaustible
treasury of insights into the moral significance of the earliest chapters of
its development. Modern scholarship in many fields of human study offers
valuable though limited knowledge of the life that was lived in the earliest,
"pre-historical" societies. A Christian is free to appropriate such knowledge, to
the extent that his individual scientific qualifications allow, and so long as he is
not deceived by claims to absolute or objective authority for the theoretical
systems undergirding these inquiries. But what we appropriate from these
explanatory sciences will add nothing to our grasp of World History, understood
as a linear process, with accumulating meanings, tending towards description of
the present world-political realities.

*Christians understand World History as the record of the ramifications
in time of the work of God in covenant with Abraham.* The story of God's
covenant with Abram is in the forefront. The background is: (a) the given state
of nature, governed by constant law, and open (in principle) to scientific
analysis and explanation; and (b) the pre-historical accomplishments of

civilization, a realm unlike that of nature, in that its life is no longer active, most of it is gone without trace, and thus not appropriable to science, now or tomorrow. When a Christian seeks instruction in the meaning of History, he is directed to this starting-point: the decision which Abram is described as making in *Genesis* 12. There is nothing to be gained by waiting while paleontologists, anthropologists, sociologists, psychologists, philologists, or other-ologists work towards construction of definitive (assured, scientific) description of the *origins* of civilization which lie perhaps millennia before this story about Abram which begins in *Genesis* 12.

We note that there are two parts to what is said in this address to Abraham:

(a) Abraham is asked to make a decision: "*Go from your country and your kindred and from your father's house ...*"; and,

(b) Abraham is given a broad but definitive promise about the consequences over the whole span of time of his decision:"*I will make of you a great nation, and I will bless you and make your name great, so that you will be a blessing ...*"

What is said in this address of God to Abraham is meaningless unless it is said from the perspective where the whole content of time is known. From this perspective, the consequences of a singular decision, made in a singular moment by a singular individual, have ramified through time and space, until they have eventually come to bring under one destiny the activities of all people everywhere in the world today. This net caches all the events of World History.

The Efficiency of Our Theory of World History.

A skeptic, approaching these claims propositionally, must at least be able to see the advantages of our theory, viewed (if possible) strictly from the point of efficiency.

Think, first, of the practical difficulties which stand before any Theory of History that passes up this starting- point. Scholars of equal goodwill differ greatly in their estimates of how long human beings have been in existence - some reckoning this span in terms of thousands, others of hundreds of thousands, others of possible millions of years, before there appear written records that give us the names of individuals, the names of the places to which they belonged, and dateable evidence of their actual deeds. Even then, those who are named in the records are an infinitesimally small fraction of all the individuals who were then in the world, let alone the presumed millions who had already left this world, and whose deeds had some bearing on the way the human adventure developed. In the absence of total documentation for the whole human population, we must not pretend that we shall ever be able to tell the whole story of mankind as a single story having a single direction. We can generalize and postulate forces at work; but we have, in honour, to keep in mind that archeological discoveries could always drastically alter the nature of the evidence, and that refinements in the theoretical-interpretative models that we bring to the ever-growing pile of evidence could potentially discredit all previous generalizations and postulates. A science of any sort builds on generalizations drawn from masses of empirical information, inductively acquired from a field of possibility presumed to be closed. But the dimensions of the long-lost human past cannot be even approximately defined. The total human content of this past of indefinable dimension is gone. There are traces - but, perversely, these are traces of the things that presumably least engaged their spirits, their ideals and their emotions. The traces are material things, made with their hands out of the toughest materials, the most commonly available materials they came across - almost always the things which, a little imagination will tell us, they cared least about. The disciplined imaginations of the various scientists of human origins wrestle with the piles of pottery shards, shells and bones, uncovered from middens (garbage-heaps). Theories are proffered about the contents of the minds and hearts of the communities who owned the garbage before it was garbage. Dogmas take hold, with respect to what may or may not be deduced regarding the family life and the religion of people who leave garbage of more and less quantities, of more and less sophisticated styles of ceramic design, appearing out of the earth in endlessly-varied juxtaposition, with infinite possibilities of permutation and combination with animal bones and human bones and bones that might be either.

In a textbook intended for college students of archeology, Robert Wenke sees the goal of archeology as "locating every prehistoric culture in time and space and arranging all of them [he quotes the archeologist Lewis Binford] 'in a way which accurately reveals their generic affinities.' " But he asks (on behalf of us outsiders to archeology) "how do you do this with prehistoric peoples who left no written records and of whom we have little more than the occasional skeleton and bags of pottery and stone?" And he answers: "The main method of culture history - and one that most archeologists still use - is to make large collections of artifacts (the things people make) from each 'site' (the houses, graves, or workplaces of ancient people) and then make a lot of brave inferences about the people who made these pots, stone tools, or whatever." He then offers "a classical example," from a dig in Iran. [10]

When my father was a boy, the most up-to-date of the scientifically-confirmed truths about the pre-historic character of mankind were all conveniently gathered in the opening chapters of a best-selling book, H.G. Wells, *Outline of History*. [11] Wells developed a distinct vision of man and man's possibilities from the generalizations then dominant in paleontology, anthropology, philology, and so on - the force of which he claimed then to be able to illustrate in action by review of the whole course of history, down to the

Great War (the War to End War). He offered up all sorts of features of pre-historic man's life at home, at play, at work, at prayer, through an exercise of imagination restrained (as he insisted) by scientific logic, playing upon the evidence from the middens. In the first edition of his *Outline*, Wells elaborated a confident Progressive, Optimistic, and Universalistic philosophy of history, which, he insisted, followed by scientific necessity from all the objective evidence, and which only the perverse could deny. However, each subsequent revision reflected some further attenuation of the optimism of the original, declining to outright melancholy by the 1939 edition. The world-view that informs the first edition of the *Outline* is now in ruins. [12] And so is most of the sociological, psychological, anthropological, paleontological, and other-logical theorizing that Wells depended upon. Wells' own portrait of Early Man was long ago hooted out of learned company. In college, the sons of H.G. Wells' young readers encountered an equally confident litany of scientific truths about pre-historic man, the lowest common denominator of which today informs the introductory sections of the college-level History of Civilization courses. It is the same straw however, and the brick is of the same quality as before.

It is simply not true that we are working our way towards a clearer, let alone a definitive, understanding of the character of pre-historic human life. Indeed, the most fundamental questions are the ones furthest from resolution. Plausible explanation for the distribution of the races around the globe in pre-historic periods is, if anything, further away than was believed in H.G. Wells' time. We are further away, not closer, to understanding the linkages among the languages of the world. We are no closer than were the ancient Greeks to answers to the debate which now takes the form: diffusion or parallel invention of culture?

It is rare to find a responsible treatment of the concepts "history/pre-history" in a textbook. One that comes close to responsibility is this, from the "Preface" to the major college text by W. L. Langer:

> The evidence for the early history of the race, is, to be sure, scanty indeed, consisting mainly of skeletal fragments and crude artifacts. No doubt there will be further finds, as there have been in Africa in recent years. But it is unlikely that the record will ever be anything but meager - too meager to enable the historian to construct even an outline story of human development. It is a sad but inescapable conclusion that by far the larger part of man's past will remain closed to the historian and continue to be the domain of the anthropologist and paleontologist.
>
> History, it has often been said, can deal only with such events as have left remains or records of some kind. This being so, it must be admitted that the time span of historical knowledge does not reach back much further than 10,000 years, for several thousand of which the evidence is sketchy to say the least ... Only the discovery and deciphering of tens of thousands of inscribed clay tablets in the Tigris-Euphrates Valley, together with somewhat latter papyri records in Egypt have within the last century and a half, given us real insight into the life of near Eastern man in times as remote as 4000 B.C. These tablets, for the most part everyday business records, were preserved merely through chance, that is, through the extreme dryness of the climate. They were never intended for the historian of the future, yet they reveal to us the existence of well-organized cities and states with highly-developed religion and literature, great artistic competence, sophisticated economic life, and elaborate legal systems. In short, for the historian human society springs fully developed out of the darkness of prehistoric time. [13]

A student would never guess this truth, however, from the cocky, strutting tone that informs the "Pre-History" chapter in most World Civilization textbooks. Typical is the semantic confusion, deliberate or inadvertent, that marks the textbook by Chodorow, *et. al.*:

> The study of world history is a comparative study of cultures [*etc.*] ... [p. xvi] As historians, we cannot speak meaningfully about the time

before history and the time after it - the time before human beings inhabited the earth and the time after this moment when the study of history begins [*sic.*] ... This process of cultural enlargement has led to a world economy ... It is the end of a cultural development, many millennia long, that began when human culture was virtually the same everywhere ... The events of human history have occurred in nearly every region of earth [*sic.*!] [14]

The project of telling the whole human story as a single story, having a single direction, on the basis of fully-accredited scientific deductions from that whole body of evidence, is a pipe-dream - one that energizes a few secular historians of a reflective sort, while the unreflecting majority of card- carrying academic historians simply bob along on its surface. That the premises of the secular model are so preposterous has done nothing of course to curtail its monopoly as textbook wisdom. Its monopoly persists because secularists guess (though few dare to think of this, and even fewer to say it out loud) that the only alternative to it is the one we are defending here: namely, the understanding of World History as the unfolding in time and over geographical space of the consequences of Abraham's decision.

We ask the skeptic: consider for a moment the impossibility of building an account of the human past on the accumulation of all the facts about the whole human adventure. Imagine, instead, that we are in a position to appoint an authority who will reach into whole human record that exists - unencumbered by paleontological, anthropological, sociological, psychological and other-logical theorizings - and who will select for us *a single recorded event*; and let us agree to make *that* our starting- point. We will then all agree, strictly in the interests of efficiency, to make *this* the story to which we will link up all the stories of all the other communities of the world, at the point where these stories link up, in time and place, with our controlling story. Since this is a fantasy in any case - let us suppose that our appointee is omniscient, that he has a record of all of human life before him - not the fragmentary record that is now in our history books, but the full record of everything that has ever happened. What principles will guide our omniscient appointee?

What he wants is an event near the beginning of the point where written records become significant in the life of human communities, since a requirement of any narrative that is going to serve as a singular and cumulative story, and which is going to be told uninterruptedly through to this present moment, is, obviously, that its earliest moments are going to have to belong to that time when a reasonably wide community of men was already capable of telling stories and committing them to writing for continuous telling and re-telling. Our omniscient appointee is looking for the *earliest literate* civilization, and for some point of time within the *earliest* chapters of that civilization, some time after writing has developed, when literacy is already widespread, at least among an elite. However long men may have been in the world prior to this point, and however "memorable" their deeds might have seemed to their contemporaries, they are not memorable to us, because there is no continuous record of the telling of their deeds that has come down to us. Nor can there be - this is a tautology! - until there is the means to write down the story and the means to perpetuate it within a continuing community. Our omniscient appointee will know at least what every informed student of World History knows today (however legitimate it may have seemed, as late as the mid-Nineteenth Century to challenge this): that there is only one candidate for this role among all the civilizations that have ever appeared in the world: and that is the civilization of ancient Mesopotamia (Assyro-Babylonia.)

Given the priority of the civilization of ancient Mesopotamia, anyone but our omniscient appointee would be tempted to proceed immediately to work his way down the chain of the successive empires which History records in this region: the Akkadian (beginning c. 2350 B.C.), the Assyrian, the Babylonian , the Persian, the Empire of Alexander, *et cetera.* The perfectly sensible thought here is that the political masters would impose their cultures, so that the cultures of the politically weak would vanish, while the master-cultures would continue to carry forward the elements of the record that we need to tell a continuous story from the earliest possible point. But, sensible though this thought may be, the facts are otherwise: none of the languages of any of the master-empires, down to and including the neo-Babylonian (Sixth to Fifth Centuries B.C.) survived as a spoken language nor as a vehicle for further literature of any kind. The last to succumb was the ancient Persian language, following the Seventh Century A.D. Moslem conquests. [15] The records of their past disappeared under the ruins of their great cities in the wake of invasion and natural catastrophe. For centuries to follow - until the Nineteenth Century in fact - such records as emerged from time to time out of the soil through archeological effort were closed to us because the languages could not be deciphered.

Our omniscient appointee knows what informed adults today know (though few pause to reflect on it, and our schools certainly invest nothing in the fact): that only one language and only one literature is available as a candidate to carry us back to the earliest hours of written history, and to carry us forward from there in uninterrupted story - and that is the Hebrew language and Hebrew literature. [16] Therefore, *If we want to tell a single, linear story, from the earliest available written documents to the present, we have to locate the origins of that story in Hebrew Scripture.* The only question is: Do we want to? There are no other candidates.

It is important to be frank about this exercise. If we wish to avail ourselves of this singularly efficient method of telling the whole story as a single story, having a single direction and accumulating meanings, occurring entirely upon the ground of human time - we have no choice but to locate the origins of the story in Hebrew Scripture. There simply is no other body of literature from the approximate time of origins of that Scripture which even purports to be able to carry *any story* forward from its own account of origins of human history to the point, centuries later, when the events with which it deals can be linked up with reliable recorded stories of other civilizations.

Most of our contemporary World History textbooks, as we have seen, begin by apologizing for the "Eurocentric bias" of their content, but then quickly get on with laying out the story on the old lines, beginning with early Sumerian civilizations; chapters which background the origins of Asian and African and pre-Columbian American civilizations typically appear somewhere near the midpoint of the book, in time to link up with the story of the foundation of European Empires in the Fifteenth Century. But some World History textbooks try a different tack around the embarrassment of "Eurocentrism." These begin by playing the visiting-anthropologist-from-Mars game with the reader, protesting that "objectively" any of the separate stories of the many separate civilizations might just as legitimately be taken as the starting-point for the recital of World History. But none of them ever actually does this. Instead, they typically spin out a few (and very difficult) introductory pages of review of recent anthropological theorizing, hinting about the laws that account for the origination of language, social and political arrangement, religion, art, and so on. According to these textbooks, science is always just on the brink of fleshing-out the dynamics of human behaviour in such thorough detail and with such authority that through retrodictive argument we will, some day soon, be able to tell the story of our origins with an authority superior to that of narrative, with the force of generalized, scientific truth. The tantalizing promise is of course that we shall soon dispense altogether with the question of chronological priority, and thus with the traditional (that is, Judaeo-Christian) narrative, and thus with World History as linear story, with accumulating meanings, occurring entirely on the ground of human time.

For purposes of our present argument: *it may be* that everything the Hebrew Scripture has to tell us about the events of the history of this tribe, down to the point where it links up with the Empires of Assyria (Eighth Century, B.C.), of Babylonia (early Sixth Century), of Persia (late Sixth Century), and then Macedonia (Fourth Century), and then Rome (First Century, B.C.) - that is, with the trunk of the tree of World History, as we must tell it) is a pack of lies. It still remains a fact of life that we cannot tell this largest story, called World History, without the history of Abraham as its prelude. Nor can we separate out the Jewish "contribution" to World History, and tell the "larger" story without it. For the fact is that the world which became heir to the Romans and the Greeks and the Sumerians and the Egyptians and Assyrians and Akkadians embraced the story of Abraham. They believed that if you followed that story through Scripture, you would see its consequences ramifying through time and space, until it created a new world of which they were the heirs and successors. They re-examined the recitals of their own previously separate pasts in the light of the story of the consequences that follow from Abraham's decision (what they called, the "Sacred History.") And they re-worked the meanings they found in those recitals (in Homer, in Herodotus, in Polybius and Plutarch and Livy and Vergil and Suetonius and Tacitus) in the new terms - the terms, eventually, of Eusebius and Orosius, and Augustine. They believed, further, that as these consequences continued to ramify, all the other nations of the world would come to see their previously separate stories fulfilled in the light of the story of the consequences of the decision of Abraham. This outcome is foreseen in God's first address to Abraham (*Gen.* 12:3), and restated by Jesus of Nazareth: "And this gospel of the kingdom will be preached in all the world as a witness to all nations, and then the end will come." (*Mt* 24:14).

Arnold Toynbee, who once virtually ruled the realm of Theory of History in the English-speaking world, expressed for his generation the resentment which post-Christian theorists of History continue to feel for the weakness shown by the Greeks and the Romans in succumbing to the Jewish spirit:

> The Christian Church, for instance, has taken over uncritically the Jewish version of the history of the Jews' predecessors, the peoples of Judah and Israel, as this is presented in the written Torah (in Christian terminology, 'the Old Testament.') Christians, and ex-Christians too, see the Phoenicians, Philistines, Edomites, Moabites, Ammonites, and Damascenes as these are portrayed in the historical books of the Torah; and they see the Seleucid King Antiochus IV and his policy as these are portrayed in the First and Second Books of Maccabees. If the Tyre and Gaza of the last millennium B.C. had living representatives to speak for them today, as Israel and Judah have, they would, no doubt, give a version of the story of their relations with the two highland communities in their hinterland which would hardly be recognizable as being an account of the events that, in the highlanders' version, are familiar to Christians from the Bible. Yet in the established Christian version of this chapter of history the Jews have things all their own way - pending the discovery by archeologist of documents written in the Syriac world, outside Judah and Israel, in the last millennium B.C. that might be of comparable historical value to the documents written in the fourteenth century B.C. that have already been unearthed at Ras ash-Shamrah. [17]

The passage just cited was written in 1961. We are still awaiting the discoveries which Toynbee anticipated for the redemption of our historiography from the link with Abraham.

Christian theologians of the formative Catholic period (roughly, the Third and Fourth Centuries) elaborated a Christian Theory of World History which they believed followed from accepting: (a), the Bible's consistent understanding of the consequences of Abraham's decision; and (b), the claim of Jesus of Nazareth that the promises made to Abraham were fulfilled in Him. As they did so, they reworked the whole story of the past in new forms, which then became the dominant forms throughout the Christian Centuries. These still stand today as the only alternatives to modern secular theories reared in explicit defiance of these premises and these forms. The founders of our Christian vision of World History - Justin Martyr (c.100-c165), Origen (c.185-c.254), Julius Africanus (c.160-c.240), Eusebius of Caesarea (c.260-c.340), Augustine (354-430), Orosius (c.380-c.420) - believed that the ramifications of Abraham's decision controlled, in a way partly hidden and partly disclosed to the eyes of faith, all the details of the political stories that coincide in time with this Sacred History. They believed that the rise and fall of political empires had been disposed by God in such a way as to create the appropriate contexts in every moment of time for the story of the unfolding of the consequences of Abraham's decision. To underline this point, they stressed the fact that all those successive political empires were gone, while the books which contain the story of Abraham and its consequences had triumphed in the world of the mind and the spirit.

I have asked the secularist to examine the advantages of telling the story of the human past in this way, believing as I do that, in terms of sheer efficiency, there is literally nothing to rival it. But of course, if one must refuse the claims that Scripture makes about the exclusive meanings of these events - in plain words: if one cannot believe that they are true - then one must, in conscience, dismiss all this as a trap. And this, in a nutshell, is the History of the Idea of History since the Eighteenth Century.

Needless to say: Christians believe that this singular possibility of telling World History efficiently is no trap, and certainly no "coincidence." Rather, it is a gift. The options are really that simple. We do not claim to have thought our way to it. We found it in the legacy of our civilization, and we prized it, and we claimed it for ourselves. We recognize that there are philosophical difficulties. But these difficulties are as nothing compared to the philosophical (let alone the moral and spiritual) difficulties that follow for Theory of History when we attempt to slough off the story of Abraham and its consequences from the recital of World History. We say that *un-mixing* World History and presenting it without Abraham and his decision and the consequences of that decision (the "Sacred History") is unscrambling an omelet. We say that the Theory of World History that informs the textbooks is denatured history. It is a theory about mankind, an anecdoted anthropology, which depends upon generalizations from the sciences and from modern natural philosophies (latterly, an unstable mix of materialistic determinism and Darwinian evolutionary biology) and which denies the possibility of telling the human past as a story with linear direction and with accumulating meanings. Seen in this light, the spirit and purpose behind the organization of contemporary textbooks in World History is precisely to destroy the meaning of World History.

"The Fraudulent Universality of Christian Histories."

"I will bless those who bless you, and him who curses you I will curse; and by you will the families of the earth bless themselves. (*Genesis* 12: 3.)" Of this, God's pledge to Abraham, Rabbi Plaut writes:

> Few biblical dicta have been more clearly reflected in history than the statement that those who bless Israel will be blessed and those who curse it will be cursed, or that those who are blessed bless Israel and those who are cursed curse Israel. The decline of a nation can often be clearly related to the way it has treated the Jew, and its prosperity stands in direct proportion to its sense of equity and human dignity. For if the Jew rests indeed at the fulcrum of spiritual history, his condition must be essential to the welfare of his environment. Enough historical evidence can be advanced - from the appearance of the Prophets to the events of the holocaust - to make a persuasive case for the archetypal significance of Jewish

existence in the world, a significance that Jews themselves have considered central ever since patriarchal days.

To be sure, the world has but rarely given credence to this view. It has not usually seen the Jews as a "great nation", typifying man's highest and noblest aspirations. Christians and Moslems have exalted Abraham as their spiritual father and at the same time have denied validity to the religious quest of the Jews. The latter, however, have stoutly maintained, through ancient, medieval, and modern persecutions, that the blessing issued to Abraham has not been abrogated, and that it is more important for the children of Abraham to be worthy of it than that others accord them recognition. [18]

But Rabbi Plaut puts this far too mildly! The case is *not* that, "The world has but rarely given credence to this view.". The case is that "this view" is deeply, fundamentally, offensive to the modern mind, and so it gives it no credence at all! Voltaire, celebrated by secularists as the man who rescued Philosophy of History from its enslavement to Religion, understood that the Bible's claim with regard to Abraham was the key to Judaeo-Christian theory of History. He would stop at nothing to belittle the reputation of Abraham. Voltaire's ridiculous reading of this history was that the Jews had appropriated the name of their alleged founder ("Abram" = "Abraham") from the Indians: it is a variation on "Brama, a son of God, who taught the Bramins the manner of adoring him ... The Jews make him come from Chaldea, and not from India and Bactria; they were in the neighbourhood of Chaldea; India and Bactria were unknown to them: Abraham was a stranger to all these people, and Chaldea being a country long famed for arts and sciences, it was an honor, humanly speaking, for a small nation inclosed in Palestine, to reckon among the number of their ancestors an ancient sage, a reputed Chaldean. If it be allowable to examine the historical part of the Judaical books, by the same rules as are followed in the criticism of other histories, it must be agreed with all commentators, that the recital of the adventures of Abraham, as it is found in the

Pentateuch, would be liable to many difficulties, if it were found in any other history." [19] The sarcasm is pitched even higher in the article, "Abraham," in his *Philosophical Dictionary*:

> Abraham is one of the names famous in Asia Minor and Arabia, as was Thout among the Egyptians, the first Zoroaster in Persia, Hercules in Greece, Orpheus in Thrace, Odin among the northern nations, and so many others known better through their fame than through any authentic history. I speak here only of profance history; as for that of the Jews, our masters and our enemies, whom we believe in and detest: since the history of that people was evidently written by the Holy Spirit, we feel about it as we should ... In fact, the race of Ishmael [i.e., the Arabs] was infinitely more favored by God than the race of Jacob. It is true that both races have produced thieves; but the Arabian thieves have been vastly superior to the Jewish thieves. The descendants of Jacob conquered only a very small country, which they have lost, while the descendants of Ishmael conquered parts of Asia, Europe, and Africa, established an empire greater than that of the Romans, and drove the Jews from their caverns, which they called the Promised Land ... The Jews, then, treat their history and ancient fables as their peddlers treat their old clothes: they turn them and sell them for new as dearly as possible.
>
> It is a strange example of human stupidity that we should have so long regarded the Jews as a nation which taught everything to others, while their historian Josephus himself admits the contrary.
>
> It is hard to penetrate the shadows of antiquity; but it is evident that all the kingdoms of Asia had been flourishing mightily, long before the vagabond horde of Arabs, called Jews, had a small spot of earth that was their own, before they had a town, laws, or a settled religion. Therefore, when we see an ancient rite, an ancient opinion, established in Egypt or Asia and among the Jews, it is natural to suppose that this small, new, ignorant, crude people, still destitute of the arts, copied the ancient, flourishing, and industrious nations as best they could. It is on this principle that we must judge Judaea, Biscay, Cornwall, Bergamo the land of Harlequin, etc.: surely triumphant Rome didn't imitate Biscay, Cornwall, or Bergamo in anything; and a man must be either a great ignoramus or a great rascal to say that the Jews taught the Greeks. [20]

In early Eighteenth century France, public expression of contempt for the teaching of the church was dangerous. Voltaire's way for winning applause while disarming the clerical censors was to package his contempt for Christian teaching as contempt for the Jews. Voltaire's instinct was correct: the best way to detach Western intellectuals from their Christian legacy was to play upon the European's resentment of the truth that World History must be understood as the record of the consequences that follow from the Promises made in a moment of time to the Father of the Jews. As the progress of atheism continued into the Nineteenth Century, it became unnecessary to disguise contempt for Christian doctrine; indeed, such expression would eventually become the hallmark of scholarly "objectivity."

That the history that follows upon Abraham's decision is (in Augustine's formulation) "the universal way" is a proposition that the academic mind simply will not listen to, and which it has in fact for two hundred years been working to put out of the court of learning and out of the realm of popular inquiry. There is nothing at all open-minded or accommodating about the attitude of modern minds when it comes to this subject. We are long past the point where the world of learning needs to feel any obligation to sit patiently while this case is made. It is established in all corners and at all levels of the world of learning today - including (indeed, especially) in the corners occupied by Religious Studies - that this case has not sufficient dignity to be entitled to be heard.

To begin with: How did this story get to be dignified as "more important" than any other story within universal human memory? Indeed: how did we ever get the idea - we, the Civilization that first found its way to science, universal literacy, government by consent of the governed, the secret of unlimited material improvement, the computer and the internet - that this story was dignified in any way at all? Voltaire and Diderot and the other luminaries of the Enlightenment were the first to discover what good fun was to be had from mocking the Church's claims regarding Abraham and the Patriarchs and the Biblical stories that follow - and at the same time (and even more significantly) that this mockery could be done with impunity, and indeed to applause. It should be noted that Voltaire believed that this fun should be confined to the ranks of people of *esprit*, the nobility of the mind; he took a dim view of anyone who thought of subverting the confidence of the masses in Christian superstitions - which confidence, he believed, was necessary for the habits of deference which in turn undergird public order. Which, in turn, undergirded the safety of his property. He would have been horrified to know that along the way of the next two centuries license to mock the Scriptures would become just another part of the democratic privilege. He never foresaw a time when the masses would learn nothing at all in their schools or in any formal way about Abraham, or Moses or David, and would know these names only as figures of fun in Monty Python skits. Yet, the fountainhead of this popular contempt for the stories of the Bible is Voltaire. It was he who set the style for mocking the Church as it went about out its task of making the adventures of Abraham, Isaac, and Jacob and that lot bear the whole Meaning of History - clearly a antic task, given that anyone looking at them with objectivity (as the *philosophes* fancied that they did) could see that they were flea-ridden nomads, made looney by too much sun and sand.

It was Voltaire and his contemporary *philosophes* who first gave currency among intellectuals to today's article of academic faith that Holy Scripture is worthless as historical material. The *philosophes* inherited a tradition of scholarly efforts - scattered at first, but settling into major schools of learning by the Seventeenth Century - to uncover the "historical reality behind the Bible" through primary philological scholarship. This led, in the Seventeenth Century, to the entrenchment of the "historical-critical method." [21]

There were pioneers in these efforts among Christians (Thomas Hobbes, Richard Simon, Jean Astruc, and J.S. Semler) and among Jews (notably, Baruch Spinoza). The Enlightenment generalized these discoveries for the learned laity, leaving out the hard parts and the qualifications, giving currency among intellectuals to the idea that the Scriptures are worthless as historical sources, and that responsible individuals must be guided by their own philosophical qualifications in appropriating only such parts of its story-materials as might seem aesthetically or morally edifying. In the early Nineteenth Century, opportunities for scholarly breakthrough into "the meanings behind Scripture" multiplied as historical skepticism rendered worthless its "external" or "superficial" meanings (those that the uneducated fed upon).

According to the "Documentary Theory," which took hold by the mid-Nineteenth Century and eventually fixed a monopoly on Biblical research and speculation in the Universities, Abraham and his contemporaries and his descendants for several generations were illiterate; generations went by while stories about Abraham and the patriarchs got transmitted orally around campfires, changing shape and emphasis, inadvertently picking up stray bits of contrary anecdote and fancy, until they came to be re-worked into definitive written form by "editors" who thrived *centuries after* Moses. Linguistic and philological expertise, they claimed, empowered the modern scholar to posit certain tendencies in the evolution of language; this plus paleontological expertise equipped him to spot anachronisms. Equipped with all these "tools," the theorists were able to determine the relative antiquity of all the "strands" of story-telling (the "Documents behind the text") and to posit the motives of all the story-tellers and of successive cohorts of "editors". Shaking off the illusion of the integrity of the text, the learned reader was now sovereignly free to find the right degree - that is, the most comfortable degree - of moral, philosophical and theological distance to take up with respect to the various parts of the Bible.

Given the working of the well-known process of "cultural lag," it has come about that the attitudes nurtured by these scholarly premises and practises eventually sifted down, so that today they appear to be the attitudes of most generally-educated lay persons who take the trouble to read or discuss Scripture. (The word "lay" in this context is used with reference to the scholarly disciplines involved in academic Biblical study, so that it would include such matters as expertise in the languages of the Bible and of theological discussion, archeology, paleontology, and Ancient History. In this sense, most clergy are of the "laity.") As is the case with cultural lag in all fields, the layman, having no access to the evidence of *current* research, nor to the history of debate that has taken place within the relevant guilds in the interim since Wellhausen, is usually unaware of the fact that the original premises are today in shambles. The Biblical historian, John Bright, summed up the situation as it stood a quarter-century ago:

> [W]hen the documentary hypothesis was developed, little was known at first hand of the ancient Orient. The great antiquity of its civilization was not even guessed, and the nature of its various cultures was scarcely understood at all. It was easy, therefore, in the absence of an objective frame of reference for evaluating the traditions, for men to doubt the historical worth of documents so far removed from the events of which they tell, and, viewing Israel in isolation against a foreshortened perspective, to posit for her earliest period the crudest of beliefs and customs.
>
> That this situation has radically changed hardly needs to be said. Dozen of sites have been excavated, and as material and inscriptional remains have come to light and been analyzed, the patriarchal age has been illumined in a manner unbelievable. We now have texts by the literal tens of thousands contemporaneous with the period of Israel's origins ... [and in the light of these] it has become clear that the patriarchal narratives, far from reflecting the circumstances of a later day, fit perfectly the age of which they purport to tell ... In addition to this, the fact that the documents, though centuries older in time [i.e., by the most "conservative" reasoning, the time of Moses, at least four hundred

years after Abraham], reflect authentically the milieu of the age of which they tell, has brought an increased appreciation of the role of oral tradition ... On the other hand, oral transmission tends to be more tenacious where writing is known and can act as a brake upon the vagaries of imagination, and where a clan organization keeps interest in ancestral traditions alive. These conditions, it may be said, obtained to a favourable degree among the Hebrews at the time when their traditions were taking shape, since the Hebrews had especially strong feelings for ties of clan and cult, and since writing was in general use in all periods of their history.[22]

Educated people today carry around the impression that the stories about Abraham and the patriarchs are taking place during a long, shapeless aeon of prelude to History, during which everyone wandered about in bathrobes. This state of affairs represents an unearned and unjustified victory for the ideology of the Enlightenment. The *philosophes* of that age attacked the received view of history for its "narrowness," and cursed the Jews for having foisted their tribal chauvinism (to use a term of later coinage) upon our whole culture. After all the long centuries of captivity to the Jewish spirit, the *philosophes* now undertook (in Peter Gay's paraphrase) to "enlarge historical space." They offered, says Gay, "a secular alternative to the theological determinism of Christian historians." In the hands of the philosophes, "the world once circumscribed by faith grew wider, older, more varied ... than it had been in the hands of Christians." [23]

Voltaire took on openly the reputation of Bishop Bossuet (1627-1704), considered the pre-eminent Christian philosopher of History, and author of the *Universal History*. In the Preface to his own universal history, the *Essai sur les moeurs*, he mocks the Bishop, who "seems to have written for the sole purpose of insinuating that everything in the world was done for the sake of the Jewish nation: that if God gave hegemony over Asia to the Babylonians, it was to punish the Jews; if God had Cyrus reign, it was to avenge them; if God sent the Romans, it was, once again, to chastise the Jews . That," he added dryly, "may be; but the greatness of Cyrus and the Romans also had other causes." [24]

For intellectuals of that generation, contempt for the Church and the Bible was sufficient motive for rejecting the Bible's picture of Abraham dutifully turning his back on civilization. But the "discovery," recently made, of the superior antiquity and longevity of the Chinese civilization gave dignity to their case against the claims of Jewish Scripture. Voltaire cried out to his contemporaries:

> Let us then [we Europeans, who are presently imposing our missionaries upon the Chinese], men merely of yesterday, descendants of the Celts who have barely cleared the forests of our savage lands - let us leave the Chinese and Indians to enjoy their lovely climate and their antiquity in peace ... [T]he constitution of their empire is in fact the best in the world, the only one founded on paternal power ... [F]our thousand years ago, when we couldn't even read, the Chinese knew all the absolutely useful things we boast of today.
> Once again, the religion of the men of letters of China is admirable. No superstitions, no absurd legends, none of those dogmas which insult reason and nature and to which the bonzes give a thousand different meanings, because they don't have any. The simplest cult has seemed to them the best for more than forty centuries. They are what we think Seth, Enoch, and Noah were; they are content to worship a God with all the sages of the world, while in Europe we are divided between Thomas and Bonaventure, between Calvin and Luther, between Jansenism and Molina. [25]

Recognizing that the world was now "wider" and "older," they now saw, as Gay puts it, that "True universal history must proceed differently":

> [I]t must begin with the oriental nations which were civilized when the West was still sunk in primitive barbarity. Voltaire carried out the program of his Preface in the body of his book: the *Essai sur les moeurs* opens with chapters on China, moves on to India, and then to Persia, a provocative instance of showing history as philosophy by examples ... Defective as his chapters on the Orient

may be [*sic!*], Voltaire wrenched the centre of history away from the Christian or the European world, and if, seeking to redress the balance, he introduced a new imbalance of his own, he showed how it might be securely established by historians better informed and less embattled than he ... Voltaire was ... making propaganda on behalf of universal history, of an attitude toward the past that embraced all civilization in the world without prejudice or parochial purpose, partly at least for their own sake, and in their own place. The philosophes were certain that authentic universality became possible only through unmasking the fraudulent universality of Christian historians - that myopic parochialism masquerading as world history.[26]

It is still today the program of secular-humanists to "wrench the centre of history away from the Christian or the European world" - a program of which Gay approves, and to which indeed his scholarly work is largely dedicated. Unfortunately for this particular "propaganda," the original effort to ground this alternative "universal history" on the priority of the Asian civilizations came to grief in the next century on the reef of modern scientific archeology. Humanist scholarship has not abandoned this position gracefully. We see something of this resentful spirit in Gay's efforts to mitigate the seriousness of the error: "[D]efective as his [Voltaire's] chapters on the Orient may be ... he introduced a new imbalance of his own." The fact is that no reliable scholar argues anymore today for the priority of either Chinese or Indian civilization - a cornerstone of the Enlightenment's theory of World History which remained in place until the latter half of the Nineteenth Century.

About the time that scientific -archeologists were establishing beyond doubt the primacy of Sumerian civilization, Georg Wilhelm Freidrich Hegel (1770-1831), gave his *Lectures in Philosophy of History* (delivered 1822-1823, but published posthumously). [27] These became the pre-eminent source for mainstream academic speculation on Philosophy of History for the latter half of the Nineteenth Century: indeed, it was still an allowable exaggeration to say, with C.J. Friedrich as late as 1956, that "An extended discussion of the influence of Hegel, and more especially his philosophy of history, would amount to a history of most learning and scholarship, excepting the natural sciences, for the last 125 years." [28] This would no longer be true today.

The starting-point of Hegel's World History is in Oriental Civilization. This appears immediately in his "Classification of Historic Data" : "The Sun - the Light -- rises in the East ... symbolizing the course of History, the Day's work of the Spirit. The History of the World travels from East to West, for Europe is absolutely the end of History, Asia the beginning, [etc]. " [29] When we get to Part One, "The Oriental World", we find: " With the Empire of China History has to begin, for it is the oldest, as far as history gives any information ... The Chinese traditions ascend to 3000 years before Christ [etc] ...." [30] In Hegel's system, everything follows necessarily ("dialectically") from the fact that man's first stirring to awareness of himself, his First grasping of the First Thought, his first confrontation with The Other, his discovery of Alienation, his going under the yoke of Religion and Government to escape fear - all this takes place in the East, where (not at all coincidentally, in Hegel's mind) the day begins (the sun rises), and nature's course, too, begins. Given the absoluteness of Hegel's claims, the system should collapse absolutely if the starting-point is thrown in doubt. That the intellectuals did not let it collapse, however, indicates how deep was the investment which the liberal-academic mind had made in it. It needs to be noted further that Karl Marx's Philosophy of History ("Dialectical Materialism") was established on this very Hegelian rock, starting with the presumed priority of Asian Civilization. Marxism's credentials as a "predictive science" are inextricably bound up in this Hegelian mechanism. We begin to see, therefore, something of the extent of the evasion which is involved in Gay's mild suggestion that "some imbalance" follows when one posits the priority of the East in the telling of World History!

We now know that the civilization within which Abraham was reared had employed writing for at least a thousand years before his time and had been using an alphabet for perhaps three or four centuries. [31] The Sumerian Civilization enjoyed continual commercial contact with the Eastern (and probably the Western) Mediterranean, Palestine, Egypt, and remoter corners of the world (present-day Libya, Arabia, and Ethiopia, and perhaps India). This state of affairs had been going on for centuries *before* the first civilization took root in the Indus Valley (that is, until about 2500 B.C.), and for yet another millennium *before* the first civilization took root in North China (that is, until about 1700 B.C.) . (These are nowadays textbook generalizations, and therefore I do not footnote them.)

Not "myopic parochialism," therefore, but the material requirements of the historical situation have determined that History must be told as the story of the consequences that follow from Abraham's decision - *if*, but only if, it is to be told as a linear story, with accumulating meanings. As this reality has dawned on the secular theorists of History, they have shifted their interests from the record of civilization (that is, the materials of history) to physical anthropology - that is the extremely fragmentary and dubious "fossilized" remains of human, "hominid", and simian skeletons. Thus, the typical World History text nowadays begins by working the anthropology textbooks for current consensus on these deposits; some deposit of manlike skeletons and putative tools in Ethiopia, South Africa, or Kenya , is then proclaimed as the starting-point of "the human adventure" or "the cradle of humanity," or something of that vague character. A generation ago, the preferred starting-point was somewhere in China. Today it is somewhere in East Africa. An admirably concise example of the current version, chosen from the Stavrianos text considered earlier, will serve for all: "During the long millennia of the Paleolithic period, *Homo sapiens* gradually scattered from their birthplace in

Africa to all the continent except Antarctica. Then the ending of the Ice Age raised the level of the oceans, thereby splitting Africa from Europe, the Americas from Northeast Asia, and Australia from Southeast Asia, to mention only the major separations. Henceforth mankind lived in varying degrees of regional isolation ... [etc.]" [32]

Whatever and wherever the particular pile of fossilized remains which is chosen to begin the story, the philosophical point is the same: We are beginning with mute, fossilized remains because the post-Christian scholar cannot find a starting-point in the historical record (which is to say, in the *written* record; which is to say, *in civilization*) for telling history as history, except the point which causes it so much and such profound chagrin - namely, the point which our Christian historiography first established, and upon which the story has been structured ever since.

In his admirable popular History of the Jews, *Wanderings*, Chaim Potok sums up the mission which the *philosophes* set for themselves:

> The men and women of the Enlightenment - in France they were called philosophes - inherited the classical writings of the Stoics and Epicureans of Greece and Rome that had been preserved by the church. They used that learning to shake themselves free of the trammels of Christianity ... [N]ow the human species stood on the threshold of a new era that was again resonant with the thought of Greece and Rome and was freeing itself of the chains of revealed religion. They were as contemptuous of Judaism as they were of Christianity .... For the past three hundred years the umbrella civilization of western man has been modern paganism, or secular humanism - secular because it has abandoned the supernatural, humanist because of its emphasis upon classical studies, or the humanities, and its regard for scientific knowledge and the worth of the individual. It is probably the most creative, the most liberated, the wealthiest, most dehumanizing, and most murderous civilization in the history of the species ... The most virulent of Enlightenment anti-Semites was Voltaire ... The central drama in the history of man, for Voltaire had not been the period of the Bible but

the time of ancient Greece and Rome. He yearned to restore that golden age of true philosophy and culture. European civilization had taken a wrong turn when it had come under the influence of Jewish and Christian ideas; it became infested with an oriental system of thought. The new age of man would return to Europe to its pure origins, re-establish its foundations in Greek and Roman antiquity.

> The ancient world had hated the Jews ... [Voltaire] recast the hatred of the Jew, put the new garb of the Enlightenment over the old ideas of Tacitus, Juvenal, Horace, and others: all men were worthy of freedom except the Jews, because the Jews were not of the same species as the rest of mankind ... He wrote, addressing himself to the Jews, "You have surpassed all nations in impertinent fables, in bad conduct, and in barbarism. You deserve to be punished, for this is your destiny" ... This feeling of contempt and disgust for the civilization of the Jews was the view of the mainstream of the Enlightenment. [33]

Today, we find the textbook writers playing their shell-and-pea game to hide the distinction between "history" and "pre-history." The true motive for this game is never declared, but it is the same as the motive that drove the *philosophes*. It is to get out from under the scandalous truth that the whole possibility of telling the story of World History stands on Christian theological premises - and that these stand upon the story that the Jews tell about Abraham and his seed.

"The Seed of Abraham."

> By faith Abraham obeyed when he was called to go out to a place which he was to receive as an inheritance; and he went out, not knowing where he was to go. By faith he sojourned as in a foreign land, living in tents with Isaac and Jacob, heirs with him of the same promise. For he looked forward to the city which has foundations, whose builder and maker is God. (*Hebrews* 11:8-10).

All historical evidence aside, the root of the offense of Jewish Scripture is that it puts the theme of civilization and its development in the background. According to this story:

(i)) Abraham turns his back on civilization ...

and we are asked by the Bible to view that as noble behaviour, which indeed God called for, and which God honours! Indeed, we are told (*Genesis* 12:1-3) that all the future meaning of History will be seen to be the fruit of this investment! To the humanist, the *meaning* of History *is* the development of civilization. Indeed, the meaning of *meaning* is the development of civilization, understood as man's autonomous and collective responsibility for the untrammeled exercise of creativity. Though the luminaries of the Enlightenment and their aristocratic patrons liked to play at re-creation of pastoral life and patronized the Noble Savage (the better to denigrate the missionary enterprise), the measure of the meaning of history was still the Progress of Civilization. This assumption, as we have seen, is fixed in the World History textbooks today.

But even this is not the end of the offense:

(ii) Abraham turns his back on civilization for the sake of reconciliation to God.

The author of *Hebrews* recalls: "These [Abraham and Sarah and Isaac and Jacob] all died in faith, not having received what was promised, but having seen it and greeted it from afar, and having acknowledged that they were strangers and exiles on the earth. For people who speak thus make it clear that they are seeking a homeland. If they had been thinking of that land from which they had gone out, they would have had opportunity to return. But as it is, they desire a better country, that is, a heavenly one. Therefore God is not ashamed to be called their God, for he has prepared for them a city"

(*Hebrews* 11:13-16).

Voltaire and Diderot and their ilk could not grasp the possibility of a civilized individual (Abraham) trading the accomplishments of culture and the dignity of urban life for promises - promises, moreover, about some far-off reconciliation of man to God - a reconciliation, that not he himself but his descendants would see. It therefore followed, in Voltaire's view, that Abraham could not be a civilized man: "He went from a country that is called idolatrous to another idolatrous country called Shechem, in Palestine. Why did he go there? Why did he leave the fertile banks of the Euphrates for a place so remote, so barren, and so stony as Shechem? The Chaldean language must have been very different from that of Shechem, which was not a place of trade; Shechem is more than two hundred and fifty miles from Chaldea; one must pass through deserts to get there. It was God who wanted Abraham to make this journey; he wanted to show him the land which his descendants were to occupy several centuries after him. The human mind has difficulty understanding the reasons for such a journey." [34] Indeed, the very notion of our needing reconciliation with God is intolerable to secularists. No better definition of *l'infame* - "superstition", the ultimate crime against man's dignity, which it was the Enlightenment's mission to "crush" (*ecraser*) - suggests itself than this picture of a civilized man walking out on human social achievement, subordinating his will to an unseen God, seeking "a better country" than any that had ever be seen on earth!

Today, scholars understand that Abraham was not the primitive individual that the Enlightenment made him out to be. Neither was he a desert nomad. He was not some narrow, untaught intelligence, grunting and sweating with the unaccustomed exercise of the newly-evolved human brain to think the First Thought about the Unseen. Nor, it should be noticed, does the Hebrew scripture depict Abraham as the founder of a new religion, nor the discoverer of monotheism. Ideas about God were all around him, abounding in all the myths and legends and pseudo-sciences and the quasi-sciences of a civilization that had been in place already for millennia. There was not one of all the possibilities of thought and deed that people think and do in the name of Religion today which was not in that world in some form that would be recognizable to our students of Comparative Religion - when Abraham walked out on that world in obedience to a direct Word, received in encounter with the One Creator God.

Blaise Pascal struck panic into the hearts of Seventeenth Century intellectuals when he told them that now and in eternity each of them would have to deal with "the God of Abraham, Isaac, and Jacob." He did not deny the large truths that the philosophers said could be known and said about God. But he had learned that true knowledge of God amounted to something other than such philosophical propositions. The Bible speaks of God Who directly addresses us in our lives, and sets before us commands which are His direct and particular will for us as individuals. Our reason, it says, is incompetent to understand why God's way is the necessary way. In the passage before us, God takes an individual out of civilization, and with that individual begins a somehow necessary work to which all study of the Origins of Civilizations gives no clue. The theme of Civilization moves to the background - or perhaps we should say to the middle-ground, the background being Nature. *The meaning of this new and necessary work is to be disclosed along the line of the consequences of this individual's singular decision in that moment of time.* These consequences will ultimately come to touch upon the lives of the whole population of the world before some final moment of time. This story carries the meaning which will ultimately result in the reordering of the whole human and natural reality - a New Heaven, and a New Earth.

"This is the universal way," Augustine says - and then immediately plunges into a *particular* study, the study of the consequences that followed in time from Abraham's decision. This infuriates the atheist. This, he protests, is no universal way! It is an utterly particular way, the particular way of a particular individual who is without any esteem for cultural accomplishment or any form of social achievement, whom we see again and again thereafter brooding about his alienation from God, never at peace, capable of noble deeds, but equally capable of despicable deceits.

But nothing that is *historically real* is either more or less than particular. We are not offended that Abraham's life is less than perfectly edifying, when the details of it are measured against some idealized propositions about the yet unrealized new humanity of the *philosophes*. We believe that Abraham's life has been redeemed under the eternal effects of the deeds in time of the life of Jesus of Nazareth, Who said of Abraham that "he rejoiced to see My day, and he saw it and was glad" (*John* 8:56.) Each particular Christian has been singularly moved by the message of the Gospel, and has, like Stephen, attached himself in his singular particularity to the promise which was given to Abraham: namely, that the outcome *in History* of his faithful decision in favour of God's command for his particular life would be the ultimate reconciliation of man to man, and man to nature and man-and-nature-together to God. The story which followed is nothing less than all the particular consequences of Abraham's decision to this present time.

We need the assistance of generalization in order to talk about this story; but this is true also about our daily life. And to get past the stage of generalized truths we need to take larger intellectual risks still and talk about patterns in History. But a faithful approach to History obliges us never to lose sight of the genuine, enduring, indeed eternally enduring, reality of the particular. All our generalizations are generalizations about massive numbers of particulars. But since we know that we cannot have access to all the facts about all the particular human lives that ever were, we accept gratefully that we have been given a particular path, on the first step of which is a particular man and a particular decision in a particular moment in a particular place; and we are told authoritatively: follow the particular consequences of that particular man's particular act. Along this path, nothing is generalized truth. There is nothing to prevent our bringing generalized truth (science, social science, philosophy) to our investigation of this pathway. But we are never to forget that the meaning of every particular soul and every particular deed described along this particular path is an eternal meaning: that is, its meaning begins along this path and concludes in eternity, which is beyond the realm of time in which the path itself lies, but is the goal of that path, the end of it, which concludes beyond time.

This vision of History is the only one that allows for absolute confidence in singular meaning and absolute confidence in the meaning of the whole story that we tell about the human experience in time. No other understanding of human meaning allows for an absolute estimation of singular human meaning without rejecting the possibilities of meaning which accumulate over time along the path of history.

(iii) Abraham turns his back upon civilization in order to found a nation.

In the Eighteenth Century, the Century of Enlightened Universalism, it was said that the Bible's message was discredited by the fact that it attached enduring, indeed apparently *eternal*, significance to nationhood. *Genesis* 9:18-29 is a key text here, as it seems to speak of national characteristics that endure from beginning to end of historical time, and a variety of historical fortunes that follow from or reflect those apparently fundamental dispositions. Much too numerous to mention are ensuing passages to the end of Jewish Scripture which speak of *God's judgement of Nations*, not only in time but in eternity. Voltaire's view, shared by all the leading luminaries, was that differences in national character and behaviour were the outcome of accidental forces only; all these differences were the effects of "custom": " It is clear that everything which belongs intimately to human nature is the same from one end of the universe to the other; that everything that depends on custom is different, and it is accidental if it remains the same. The empire of custom is much more vast than that of nature; it extends over manners and all usages; it sheds variety on the scene of the universe; nature sheds unity there." [35]

If there is only one form of reason (the sufficient-critical reason which is fundamental to human nature); and if this form of reason is universal, provided out of General Issue to everyone, everywhere - it follows as the night the day that, as men everywhere are liberated from their various superstitions, their behaviour everywhere will become more uniform. Enlightenment will "shed unity."

And, when it came into power, it did. The Revolutionary regime of the 1790's, and then the Emperor Napoleon, imposed their secular-rational understanding upon the disorderly "customary" ways of all the European nations who came within their Empire - to the great rage of these nations, who, after their eventual liberation, were gripped by "reactionary" Nationalism. Many of the most important elements in the Eighteenth Century intellectual's creed were now put out of fashion: the notion that the purest reason was critical reason, the notion that customary differences were accidental and ephemeral. The Nineteenth Century became the Age of Romantic Nationalism.

Despite an immediate impression that Christian faith had recovered prestige in the post-Napoleonic age, it soon became clear that the long-range tendency was still in the direction of secularism in all realms of life. Specifically (with reference to our present concern), the intellectuals' contempt for Abraham and God's alleged "promises" grew apace. Whereas it was the Bible's extreme attachments to the enduring meaning of "nations" that infuriated the Eighteenth Century, now, in the Nineteenth Century, it was charged that the Bible tended to *discredit* "Nationalism" (now agreed to be the most important, the most enduring, the most "scientifically" real principle in life) by trying to make out that its perfect embodiment was the Jewish race! [36]

(iv) Abraham turns his back upon civilization in order to found the Nation of Israel.

The Universal Way is the way of an individual - the way of Abraham. It is equally, and without contradiction, the Way of a community: the Nation of Israel. Nineteenth Century "Romantic Nationalists" were enthusiastic about their "discovery" of the importance of inherited communities of all kinds - clans, and tribes, and races. As the century wore on, their greatest attachment became the greatest community - the Nation-State. They became fixated on the issue of what constituted "Greatness" in the Nation. All the theorizing that supported the new spirit of nationalism had one great negative premise which constituted its lowest common denominator: Greatness in a Nation is the *opposite* of what the Bible claimed was the greatness of the seed of Abraham! How could anyone with an iota of knowledge of World History believe that History had borne out the alleged Promise of God to Abraham: that he would make him a great nation? *"All the families on earth will pray to be blessed as you are blessed!"* When, in the intervening centuries, had Great Nations wished to be blessed as the seed of Abraham was blessed? Where in the world today (the Nineteenth Century) was there any nation that would trade its destiny for that of the seed of Abraham? Was it not obvious that, taking it all in all, the story of the seed of Abraham was a story of humiliation?

True: the record of this nation of Israel is not glorious. It had nothing about it that would attract the emulation of anyone in the Nineteenth

Century who cared for the present or the future greatness of France, Germany, Italy or Russia, and nothing to teach those devoted to the recovery or the establishment of the national dignity of Poland, Spain, Denmark, Norway, Sweden, Ireland, Serbia, Croatia, Bohemia, Bulgaria, Latvia, Esthonia, or Lithuania. The option is clear: to affirm the meaning of the Promise to Abraham on the Bible's own terms is necessarily to devalue absolutely and radically the apparent, the *evident*, meanings of History. The thought took hold eventually that to affirm this alleged Promise to Abraham was to subvert the plain meaning of all study of History, and thus to stand as an enemy to the realization of all the rightful political goals of enlightened people.

No one challenged the truly astonishing fact of the survival of the Seed of Abraham. In fact, secularists were quick to concede that this was an unparalleled story. But they denied that it was a glorious accomplishment. The fact that it was unique gave away the truth that the Jews were not a people like other people, not a people in any of the senses that made being a Nation a glorious thing. Thus the early Christian and medieval gravemen against the perfidious Jews was now overlaid by a much more dangerous strain called "anti-Semitism" - more dangerous because it carried the prestige of modern philosophy and science.

We cannot be serious about our Christian faith unless we affirm the Promises that God made to Abraham. And we cannot do this without affronting everything that the modern mind thinks it knows about the meaning of history. Still, we risk saying that the Promise of *Genesis* 12:1-3 gives us our principles for the organizing of the whole human story as a story of linear direction, with accumulating meanings. We have argued that apart from this Promise there is no way in reality to organize the human story, as a linear story, with accumulating meanings. But we have to understand the corollaries to all of this. It is obvious that this story cannot be told as a story of political triumph. Israel never takes up a place in the front or even the middle rank of political significance. The nearest she comes to it is in the latter part of the reign of David and during the reign of Solomon, when she was the dominant national community in the politics of her *immediate* neighbourhood - a period of perhaps a half-century, when both Egypt and Assyria/Babylonia were in some internal turmoil. Thereafter, the nearest she came to that moment, was during the less-than-a-century of national autonomy under the Maccabees (142 B.C. - 63 B.C.), ending in the humiliation of swift annexation to Rome's empire (63 B.C.).

Thus, we will not find an "objective" vindication of this blessing of Abraham and his seed if we take the measure of political power. Instead, we start with the fact that puzzles and offends the secularists: the *persistence* of Israel. Objectively speaking, the persistence of Israel is owing to her being an exception to all the rules of survival and persistence which have governed the destinies of other nations. The community of Israel is still alive, and no community whose origins are contemporary to hers is anywhere to be seen. (We shall have more to say on this theme in Chapter Six.)

Adding to the mystery of the persistence of the Seed of Abraham is the fact that World History has, in the interim, taken shape - much as the pearl takes shape around the parasite or the grain of sand that has found its way into the interior of the oyster - around this unique and two-fold mystery of Israel's political humiliation and spiritual triumph. We say that apart from this mystery, there is no principle for organizing history as a linear story, eventually incorporating all the discrete stories of mankind's many civilizations.

Chapter Three: What Jesus Taught About Himself And About History.

Who He Is.

We are told in John's account of Jesus' life that there came a day, during His ministry in Galilee, when His brothers urged Him to go up to Jerusalem openly, accompanied by the masses of those who were declaring their allegiance to Him because of His teaching and His healing. Commentators understand the brothers' motivation in various ways. Some, noting that His brothers are never included among His believers prior to His resurrection, [*Mt* 13:55, *Mk* 3:21; and cf. *I Cor* 15:7]), suspect that their secret thought was to be rid of Him. They knew that "the Jews" (that is, the religious and political leaders at Jerusalem) "sought to kill him" [*Jn* 7:1]. Other commentators, concluding that the brothers did at least wish Him well, suggest opposite motivation: that the brothers looked forward to the dignities that would belong to them as His natural family when the authorities submitted, as the people of Galilee seemed to be doing, to His greatness, making Him some gift or other of real ecclesiastical, perhaps even political, power. The matter of their motivation does not, however, seem to have been of any interest to John, who tells the story.

Jesus' answer is: "My time [Καιροσ =kairos] has not yet come, but your time is always here .... Go to the feast yourselves; I am not going up [some manuscripts read: "I am not yet going up"] to the feast, for my time has not yet fully come" (*Jn* 7:6, 8). "But after his brothers had gone up to the feast, then he also went up, not publicly but in private" (*Jn* 7:10).

Here Jesus makes claim to knowledge of a sort that no sane individual has ever claimed. He claims to speak from knowledge of *the whole content of time*. Many individuals in the Old Testament claim to have insights (always presented as messages from God) into *some part of* the content of future time. (We will be developing this theme later, in Chapter Five.) All the prophets make such claims, as do various seers and soothsayers, not all of whom are recognized by scripture as the designated voices of the God of Israel. These insights vary in character. Some have to do only with the general shape of the future; others tell something about an important aspect of the future situation, that the hearers must be prepared for; occasionally (but more rarely), we are told about a specific item of future fact that we must be ready to understand and act upon when we meet it. But no one in the Old Testament claims that he knows what he knows and is able to say what he says because the *whole content* of the future is open to him. Jesus does claim this.

To make clear the uniquely sovereign attitude that He is assuming towards time and its content, He contrasts his situation with that of his brothers (and, logically, with all men). *My time has not yet come*. The great events that belong to His life have fixed times assigned to them. [1] *In their true character*, these great events are not to be understood as the outcomes of other events. But as for His brothers: *your time is always here*. That is, His brothers may set out for the city, and along the way be detained by all kinds of accidental situations ("accidental" in the philosophical sense), which will have the effect of altering or adjusting the time of their arrival, or perhaps preventing their arrival altogether.

My life, and that of everyone else, is like that of Jesus' brothers. There is no way of understanding the outcome or any of the details of my life-history without reckoning in all other life-histories of all the other individuals who cross my path. My life-history is governed by the total effects of all the other life-histories. Jesus' life-story is *essentially* different. No detail of any other life stands in "accidental" (again, in the philosopher's sense) relation to any detail of His life. His life-story is *governed* by nothing. His life-story is the one life-story that is all essence, no accident. It is timed, in all its detail. In *Lk* 13:31-3, for example, we read: "At that very hour [on the same day= Ev αυτη τη ημερα]some Pharisees came, and said to him, 'Get away from here, for Herod wants to kill you.' And he said to them, 'Go and tell that fox, "Behold, I cast out demons and perform cures today and tomorrow, and the third day I finish my course. Nevertheless I must go on my way today and tomorrow and the day following; for it cannot be that a prophet should perish away from Jerusalem." ' "

The timing of Jesus' trial, His crucifixion, and His resurrection have all to fit perfectly the requirements of His function as the Christ (Messiah). There is a script which His actions follow. The script is written by God. There is no element of human program in it. The Prophets did not write this script, but were only given glimpses. The prophets did not invent the role which Jesus plays. But as Jesus lives it out, it will fulfill perfectly everything that they were given to see and to proclaim. Nothing will deflect him a hair to one side or other of perfection in fulfilling it. We must not think of Jesus watching, as it were, the activities of all around him, and timing his deeds to fit these circumstances; His sovereign behaviour is in total conformity of Purpose with His Father. [2] Jesus acts, and the act *belongs*, because all of History prior to this act has been put in place for him to act right there, at that moment, precisely like that, precisely with those words, precisely before that very audience. And it belongs, equally, because all that will follow from the act, until the end of the ages, is already known and is in place. From the perspective of eternity - from which the whole content of time is known - it has all already happened: these future consequences are as much as part of the whole content of time as the events of the past, which are we describe as its "causes.".

His Perspective on Time.

On the way to Gethsemane, after His Passover supper with the disciples (*Mk* 14:26f, and synoptic parallels: *viz, Mt* 26:30f, and *Lk* 22:39f), He foretold, out of His knowledge of the whole content of time: "*You will all fall away; for it is written, 'I will strike the shepherd, and the sheep will be scattered'*" (*Mk* 14:27, citing *Zechariah* 13:7). That they will behave this way is already known to Him. Likewise, it was already, somehow, in some sense, known to Zechariah, who had been given a message from God for the people of Israel which speaks of these very events, which Jesus is now about to live out. Zechariah *was* some five and a half centuries from these events; Jesus *is* now, in the instant that He utters these words, a few hours away from them. This is how we, as singular individuals, living in time, must conceive and speak of these things. Yet, in another sense, Zechariah and Jesus are equidistant from these events, which are to each of them future, and thus not yet in the realm of time, when either of them speaks. Yet both know these events to be absolutely real - as real as the events which they have already experienced in their singular lives.

Yet, a few minutes later, Jesus is speaking as though none of this need happen - the trial, the crucifixion, the flight of the disciples - as though the future is still radically open, and has no content in it; for, "going a little further, he fell on the ground, and prayed that if it were possible, the hour might pass from him. And he said, 'Abba, Father, all things are possible to thee; remove this cup from me. ' " (*Mk* 14:35-6). But here, we note, He is speaking to God. This is a conversation within the triune consciousness of God. The challenge for our reason and for our faith lies in the fact that Jesus is not presented in the Gospels as speaking consistently from the perspective of eternity - that is, the perspective from which the whole content of the past and the future is open. We are told, for instance, that when he learns of the execution of John the Baptist, he is apparently as unprepared as the others, and changes his plans (*Mt* 14:12-13). Yet, on another occasion, still in the midst of his Galilean ministry, he announces suddenly to his disciples, "I saw Satan fall like lightening from heaven" (*Lk* 10:18). But Satan had not fallen! If, as we are taught, Satan's fall was accomplished by Christ's death and resurrection, Jesus is out of order in announcing Satan's fall already! Even now, nineteen and a half centuries later, we are out of order in announcing Satan's fall, even though Christ has since died and risen. But we are told to announce this, and we do; and in so doing we claim, on the authority of those events, knowledge that belongs only to those who have seen something from the perspective of eternity, where the whole content of time, including its conclusion, is seen.

To my knowledge, Oscar Cullmann comes as close as any theologian has ever come to expressing what can be expressed about this mystery: how Jesus, God Incarnate in Man, should be understood as sharing in the knowledge that God has of the whole content of time, while living genuinely within the limits of creaturely-human life-in-time:

> Only to him [God] does eternity belong. He is the Lord over the ages (I Tim. 1:17). Thus his Lordship is shown in the fact that he alone knows the *kairoi* or seasons of his redemptive action, that he

alone knows *the* day and *the* hour, which are unknown to "the angels in heaven" and even to "the Son" (Mark 13:32) ... Thus I Cor. 2:7 speaks of "God's wisdom, the hidden wisdom, which God has *fore*ordained from eternity to our glory." Thus the Son, who carries out this redeeming work for men, is with God from the beginning. "Before the foundation of the world." God loved him (John 17:24). Christ is already "foreknown," before the foundation of the world (I Peter 1:20), as a sacrificial lamb, and in the creation of the world its Redeemer already takes part.

   Although, as we have heard [i.e., Mk 13:32] Christ in his incarnation does not share in God's knowledge concerning the day and the hour, yet through his revealing and redeeming work he is the bearer of God's Lordship over time. In him the entire redemptive time can be surveyed. Hence it results that where Christ acts the future process is already determined ... Those raised from the dead, the young man at Nain and Lazarus, must indeed die again, for they have not yet been raised to a "spiritual body." And yet in the presence of Jesus death has already lost its sovereign power over them ... [Thus, the Gadarene demoniac complains to Jesus:] "Have you come here to torment us *before the time?*" (Matt. 8:29). The demoniacs themselves thus note that here, even before the time, a decision is made whose effect for the kingdom of Satan still lies in the future. [3]

The authors of the Gospels never seek to develop this reality propositionally. They offer no formula. Instead, they tell the story as they or their sources saw and heard it. And, out of the narrative, the truth of the matter of Jesus' unique nature presents itself as a mystery to be embraced and cherished, or as an anomoly to be rejected.

The Sign of the Times.

There is no avoiding the comprehensive and exclusive nature of the claims that Jesus made for Himself, and which Christians must repeat on His behalf, if they are not to be guilty of evasion. What struck His contemporaries most powerfully was His claim of a sovereign authority over the processes of nature - the open secret behind His power to heal, to revive the dead, to calm the storm, to multiply the loaves and fishes. But even more extraordinary was His claim to sovereignty over the processes of History. Towards the end of his Galilean ministry, "... the Pharisees and Saducees came, and to test him they asked him to show them a sign from heaven. He answered them, 'When it is evening, you say, "It will be fair weather; for the sky is red." And in the morning, "It will be stormy today, for the sky is red and threatening." You know how to interpret the appearance of the sky, but you cannot interpret the signs of the time. An evil and adulterous generation seeks for a sign, but no sign shall be given to it except the sign of Jonah.' So he left them and departed "(*Mt.* 16:1-4).

They came seeking "a sign." What, in fact, did they want? They wanted a "miracle", a demonstration on command of some wonderful departure from the expected in the realm of nature. They knew He had been providing wonders of this kind; there had been many healings, including reports of restoration from death, reports of commanding the weather to change, two incidents of the multiplication of loaves and fishes. Some of their ranks had witnessed some of these wonderful events; but these witnesses had been challenged when they told their reports to the others, and we can assume that doubts had begun to take shape in the minds of the witnesses themselves. If, here and now, Jesus will provide a spectacular "sign" of His power over the processes of nature, the issue of His alleged authority over nature will be resolved. Why will He not oblige them?

He replies, in effect: nature is full of signs. It is governed by regularities (A modern mind would speak of "laws", as would some Greek philosophers.) He reminds them: You have a certain confidence in regularities of nature, on the basis of which you make your plans: "you interpret the appearance of the sky" (NKJV: "You discern the face of the sky.") Then he told them a parable: "Look at the fig tree, and all the trees; as soon as they come out in leaf, you see for yourselves and know that the summer is already near" (*Lk* 21:29-30). In *John* 4:35, He says to His disciples: "Do you not say, 'There are still four months, then comes the harvest?' I tell you, lift up your eyes, and see how the fields are already white for harvest!' " In *Luke* 12:54, "He also said to the multitudes, 'When you see a cloud rising in the west, you say at once, "A shower is coming;" and so it happens. And when you see the south wind blowing, you say, "There will be scorching heat;" and it happens.' " Here He is teaching a lesson from everyday understanding. We watch for familiar signs from nature. These give us evidence of stages in nature's time. (We think of the item of folk wisdom: "Red sky at night; fisherman's delight!")

So far, the thought is merely a truism. Was Jesus evading the challenge of the Pharisees? Perhaps some readers of the Gospel might miss the point, and see in this the dodge so well-known in the "Does God Exist?" Debate. The agnostic or atheist says: "Do you really believe in all those miracle-stories: Jesus walks on the water, turns water into wine, heals instantly blindness, leprosy; He raises the dead ...!?" And the University Chaplain, the spokesman for the "faith side," smiles indulgently, and purrs: "Isn't the greatest miracle of all nature itself???"

But Jesus is not evading their challenge. On the contrary, He is dramatically escalating the stake. He is announcing that He is embarked on the project of performing the greatest *"signs"* conceivable - the *"signs of the times."* He is not denying His questioners' premises: namely, that signs (in the sense of acts which demonstrate an ability to circumvent or abridge the regularities of nature) are possible. Nor does He deny that He has performed numerous examples of these. Indeed, He will later perform even greater ones. Nor is He here denying their piety. He concedes their piety in "looking to the sky" for signs, [4] and agrees with them that God's sovereignty is demonstrable in the laws of nature. What, then, is the point of these truisms about "the signs of nature/heaven"?

In every case, we find that the context of the apparently truistic instruction is a message about the course of the Sacred History. Whether speaking to the insiders (that is, the disciples [*Jn* 4:35]) or to the hostile outsiders (that is, the Pharisees [*Mt* 16:1-4]), the device is the same: He teaches that the reason that they have for confidence in the regularities of nature is well-founded, and ought to serve as example for an equivalent confidence in the signs which Jesus is teaching them and living out before them regarding the fulfillment of the Sacred History. Jesus refuses to work a nature-miracle on this occasion, here and now, on their command. The purpose of any "signs" that might be addressed to them would be to meet the needs of their recipients. A sign from natutre - a "miracle" - would not meet the needs of the Phariesees.

As teachers of Israel, the Pharisees are accustomed to proclaim the God of Israel to be the Creator and the sustainer of the whole natural order. What the Pharisees are neglecting is that this same Creator-God has a Plan which *precedes* Creation - a Plan for the redemption of men and of nature from the curse which is at the root of man's alienation from man, and man's alienation from nature, and the alienation of man-and-nature-together from God. Jesus is saying: consider all the deeds that I have done to this point, and watch me closely from this moment forward, and you will see me performing *the signs of the times*.

Nature and History.

At the same time that he draws Pharisees' attention to these signs, Jesus foresees that they will miss them, for the same reason that they missed the signs of His authority over nature. The work on which He is embarked - the origins of which they have seen, the conclusion of which they shall shortly see - can be understood *by analogy* from the work of nature. Thus, the apparent truism that we watch "the fig tree and all the trees, and when they are already budding, we see and know for ourselves that summer is near," is really "a parable" (*Lk* 21:29). What makes it a parable is the continuation: "So also, when you see these things taking place, you know that the kingdom of God is near. Truly, I say to you, this generation will not pass away till all has taken place" (*Lk* 21:31-32). The accomplishment of the Kingdom of God, which is the work of the Sacred History, is like the natural processes, in that:

- it has its origins;
- it goes through stages;
- it culminates in the bearing of fruit;
- it proceeds according to laws.

This work accomplishes the purposes that God has put in place for man's good (as fruit is for man's good). (The fig, it should be recalled, is in the Old Testament typically associated with prosperity, and also with prophetic warnings). [5] We do not understand the processes which underlie either the origins or the growth or the fruition of the figs. But we do recognize the signs that we are given. *All that we need to know* can be read from signs which are external to these purposes, and objectives. But there is a profound difference between the signs that govern our dealings with the fig tree, and the signs of the times. We recognize the former, because we have seen them again and again, as have our father and their fathers, back to the original generations. The signs of the times, however, do not belong to a class or genus. They do not happen again and again. There is only one Plan of Redemption, and *one sequence of singular dealings of God with Israel.* The wise man goes to science for knowledge of the ways of nature. For knowledge of the Kingdom, he goes to the Sacred History.

Jesus draws the attention of His hearers to nature, and examines their attitude toward nature, because he wishes to teach them about the Sacred History which He is fulfilling. They must grasp that the latter is like the former, in that it is under God's sovereignty; it is therefore orderly, its outcome is sure. They must likewise grasp that it is *unlike* the processes of nature in that all its events are singular, and therefore there is no prior access to its unfolding, neither to its general shape nor to its detail, by the method of science, which proceeds from observation, to generalization, to predictive law.

It is because the sacred History is both like and unlike the processes of nature, that speaking of nature yields parables about the Sacred History.

"Before Abraham Was, I am."

"An evil and adulterous generation seeks   for a sign, but no sign shall be given it except the sign of Jonah" (*Mt* 16:4).

On   this, or perhaps another similar occasion   (cf.   *Mt* 12:38-42), he amplified the reference to the "sign of Jonah": "For as Jonah was three days and three nights in the belly of the whale, so will the Son of man be three days and three   nights in the heart of the earth. The men of Ninevah will arise at the judgement with this generation and   condemn it; for they repented at the preaching of Jonah, and behold, something greater than Jonah is here. The queen of the South will arise at the judgement with this generation and condemn it; for   she came from the ends of the earth to   hear the wisdom of

Solomon, and behold, something greater than Solomon is here " (*Mt* 12:40-42).

We need to reflect here, before proceeding further, on Jesus' attitude towards the Scripture of His time - i.e., what we call the Old Testament. All the biblical characters whom He mentions - for example, in this text, the Queen of Sheba and Solomon, and elsewhere David, [6] Elijah, [7] Abraham, [8] Jonah, [9] and Daniel [10] - apparently exist for Him in the same plane. All are for Him "historical", and all are "signs". At one time or another, they all lived in time and place: now they all live with God, for God is not God of the dead but of the living (*Mt* 22:32). He does not think, as liberal scholars do, that some are historical, while others are symbols or types or metaphors or eponymns, or perhaps partake of these several qualities. He seems to presume the "historicity" of each character He names, and, relying on the record of their behaviour in Scripture, He presumes to make observations about them as we do of characters in our History books. But He also claims to know each of them in a context which is totally beyond us. It is not that they are ghosts or spirits or familiars. He seems to see their whole earthly existence in eternity. [11]

In one of His confrontations with the Pharisees (*John* 8), Jesus warns them of their need to be "made free" (*Jn* 8:32). The religious leaders deny that they have any need to be made free by anyone, for "We are Abraham's descendants, and have never been in bondage to anyone" (8:33). But Jesus replies that their hostility to Him is inconsistent with their being children of Abraham, since it is out of character with Abraham (8:40). They are therefore in bondage to sin, like everyone else (8:34). Enraged at His presuming to explain Abraham's character to them, they retort: "Abraham is dead and the prophets ... Are you greater than our father Abraham, who is dead? And the prophets are dead. Whom do you make yourself out to be ...? " (8:53).

Jesus' answer is breath-taking: "Your father Abraham rejoiced that he was to see my day; he saw it and was glad." The Jews then said to him, "You are not yet fifty years old, and have you seen Abraham?" Jesus said to them, "Truly, truly, I say to you, before Abraham was, I am." (8:56-8) [12] Here Jesus makes His categorical and exclusive claim to the perspective on History which belongs to the Creator. He *was* before Abraham, because He *was* before Creation! And knowing what is to be known from the perspective of the Father-Creator, He is able to say what no mortal could claim to know: that Abraham both *had* and *has* knowledge of this day. Abraham's life-in-time moved towards these events which make up Jesus' life-in-time; but Abraham's life-in-time ended hundreds of years before. These events of Jesus' life are about to be revealed as the fulfillment of the meaning of the history of the Covenant, which Abraham's life-in-time set in motion (cf. *Hebrews* 11:8-20). We know that Abraham in his life-in-time did not see this day. But Jesus portrays Himself (Who *is* before Abraham was born), looking now upon Abraham, who in turn is looking back from his place in eternity, with God, upon the completion of the work of the Covenant - which work (as Jesus of Nazareth speaks) is still future!

It is in the light of these claims that we have to reflect on the "sign of Jonah".

What does it mean that Jonah is a sign? In its normal sense, a sign signifies: it points to other meanings than the literal in-context meaning. In the vocabulary of literary studies, Jesus is using allegory. The story of Jonah's experience inside the great fish signifies, He says, the burial and resurrection of Christ (*Mt* 12:40). Thus, in addition to and quite apart from all the meanings the teachers of Israel have seen in the story, Jesus gives the story a new significance. As Jesus explains it, the story points to meanings which could not have been seen by Jonah, who lived it, nor by the authors of the text who wrote it. Nor had these meanings been seen by anyone hearing the story down to this moment, when Jesus offers them. Furthermore, even those to whom He is presently speaking cannot see this new meaning, which sounds like some kind of riddle - until it is fulfilled, in the burial and resurrection of Jesus. Then its meaning will be clear. It is a sign of the resurrection of Jesus.

Jonah's story serves as an interim embodiment, for all who have spiritual insight, of the whole purpose of history. Jonah, who was a servant of God's largest Purpose - the reconciliation of mankind to Him - cannot, despite his conspicuous unworthiness (his reluctance, his grudging and resentful spirit), resist service as a premonition of the ultimate embodiment (the Incarnate Son of God) of God's saving Purpose in History. This ultimate embodiment will reveal perfectly what Jonah, in his adventures, reveals imperfectly, indeed almost comically. Jonah was a sign, a sign to the Ninevites: on instructions of the God of Israel, he brought the message that they were to repent. But Jonah is also a sign to Israel: he brought the message reluctantly, because he did not want to share either the bad news (that God requires repentance) or the good news (that God delivers those who do repent) to the *goyim*. The book of *Jonah* ends with the prophet sulking and cursing his life, because of the success of his mission! He is "angry enough to die!" (*Jonah* 4:9b). God will reach all mankind with His message, requiring repentance of all, offering salvation to all. He will accomplish this not grudgingly (like Jonah) but as a totally self-sacrificing hero. He will be captured by the Adversary of His Purpose (as was Jonah by the great fish). He will be hopelessly captured. He, the Son of Man, will die - not apparently, but really; he will be captured and then dead. But, as Jonah was three days in the belly of the whale, so will the Son of Man be three days and three nights in the heart of the earth.

We must assume, given Jesus' "literalistic" attitude towards the story (to use the vocabulary of Twentieth-Century theological debate), that He is requiring us to believe that God put Jonah through this particular trial for reasons that surpassed all the reasons that the actual text (the book of *Jonah*) talks of, and all the reasons that the teachers of Israel, including those present, could see. It is only from God's own perspective - that is, from the perspective where the whole content of time is known - that such things can be shown.

On Jesus' view, the voices we hear speaking in the Bible express more than they can know about the unfolding of God's Plan, the Plan which is to be accomplished through History. When subsequent generations come to see that very enactment in History of events to which the Old Testament voices are alluding, they will understand better than that voice (in this case, the voice of the author of the *Jonah*) what he himself is saying. It is therefore legitimate, it is right, it is *required* of Christians to "read into" the Old Testament foreshadowing's of Christ's work. We never see Jesus willfully adjusting or adapting His actions to "fulfill prophecy." *His actions in His lifetime are the causes of the prophecies.* His sovereignty in this process is behind His claim to tell the teachers of Israel the meaning of Jonah as a sign. He alone knows this meaning, which belongs to the future as He speaks, but which nonetheless governs or shapes the adventures of Jonah.

The difficulties that follow from allegorical uses of Scripture can be immense. But in essence the issue is simple, and urgent: do we, or do we not, follow the lead of Jesus as an exegete of Scripture? He stood clearly in the tradition of the Teachers of Israel in proclaiming allegorical meanings from Scriptural texts. He affronted the Teachers of His time in declaring these *new* allegorical meanings: their doctrine was that all the possible allegorical uses of Scripture had been fully uncovered and the catalogue of these was as strictly closed as was the canon of Scripture itself. Still, the affront to doctrine of offering new allegorical meanings was as nothing compared to the fact that, in the same breath, *He applied these meanings to Himself.* He saw and proclaimed Himself as the complete outcome of all the prophetic signs of the Old Testament. He based this claim upon the prior claim that He was in His own Person the Inspirer of the prophecies! Thus, there are rhythms and patterns in the adventures which figure in the sacred history (the Old Testament History of Redemption) which owe their significance to the *future* course of the Incarnation.

Much caution should accompany all our study on this theme. But we will not go far wrong, in my view, if we take the lead of the earliest theologians, beginning with Paul and the author of the *Letter to the Hebrews*, then the Church Fathers (Justin, Irenaeus, Clement of Alexandria, Origen, Eusebius, Jerome, and Augustine.) And we cannot go wrong at all if we take the explicit "exegesis" of Jesus - as, for example, in this present text about Jonah. So, following this teaching of Jesus, we say that Jonah was a sign pointing to Jesus: his adventures were, so to speak, shaped by God to be an adumbration of Jesus' adventures. Three days captive in the belly of the whale: three days hidden away in the earth. No one should pretend to grasp all of what is being said here. But equally, no one should refuse to accept gratefully what is clearly said and plainly accessible.

Jonah in his lifetime was a sign to the Ninevites - an emissary or messenger of God, a human witness to the power of God, a declarer of His will. The Ninevites are commended by Jesus for hearing out this witness, and acting according to the message which they saw and heard: they repented. In the same sense, Solomon was a sign to the Queen of Sheba (*Mt* 12:41 -42). There are interesting points of contrast between these two stories. Ninevah is a community of people, the people of the capital of Assyria. Collectively, they saw and heard and repented. The Queen is an individual, who saw her need for wisdom, and is here praised for seeking it out, carrying it back to her people. The Queen represents the most remote of all the nations that the people of ancient Israel had any knowledge of. [13] In Jonah's time, by contrast, Israel was divided and vulnerable: the Northern Kingdom would, indeed, disappear into the Assyrian Empire; while the Southern Kingdom was weak and slated to go at the next political cycle into the Empire of Babylon, Assyria's successor. In the Queen's time, Israel was at the height of its significance, when it was most prosperous, most renowned (which is the point of the story), most admired, most free, in charge of her destiny. The Ninevites are initially passive: the message is brought to them, missionary fashion; they hear, and they repent, and they are praised for this. The Queen, in contrast, is active throughout: she seeks out wisdom at some pain and cost; it is Solomon (Israel) who is passive. The more one looks at it, indeed, the more one is struck by the complementarity of the two sets of figures. On the one side, Ninevah, in the Jonah story, is a nation which is sought out, which is strong and proud, historically central, in charge. On the other, the Queen in the Solomon story is an individual, the surrogate of a nation which is remote, historically insignificant or peripheral (*"she came from the ends of the earth."*) Jesus has brought these two stories together precisely for this effect. They belong together as a *merism*: i.e., a conjunction of opposite ideas or characteristics so as to suggest totality.

If Jonah's three days in the belly of the great fish corresponds to the three days of Jesus' burial, concluding in resurrection, then it seems to follow that Jonah's subsequent "adventures" as a preacher speak allegorically of the outcome of the New Testament story: that is, of the dissemination of the message of Jesus by His Church. And since Jesus has associated in His praise the repentance of the Ninevites and the discovery of wisdom by the Queen of Sheba, He is telling us something about the totality of the Church's missionary history. Ninevah and the Queen of Sheba, the populations of great communities and individuals seeking wisdom, the passive and the active, the near and the far, the central and the peripheral - all the nations will in time be confronted by the sign which Solomon and Jonah so differently prefigure. For these two also constitute a merism: the wise and powerful and admired and strong King of the hour of Israel's greatest strength, and the miserable, reluctant, prophet of the time of Israel's humiliation. We are told that the men of Ninevah and the Queen of Sheba will "arise at the judgement," and so will this generation (the generation of Jesus' hearers). And - a truly shocking idea for these hearers! - the men of Ninevah and the Queen of Sheba (all the nations and individuals who repent) will "condemn" this generation of Jews!

Again, none of this talk has any possible authority or even any usefulness unless Jesus is speaking from the perspective where (when) the whole content of history is known. The judgement of which Jesus speaks is future to the people of Ninevah and the Queen, and to all the prophets who spoke of the final judgement, including the latest, John the Baptist. And it was future to Jesus of Nazareth as He spoke that day. And so it is still to us as we read all this.

The stakes here seem obvious. If Jesus knows these things, He knows them absolutely: He knows them from the perspective from which the whole course and content of History is known. If this is the case, we are being told something about the shape of World History in its unfolding. We should be ready to pay any price to know what can be known from that perspective. And, as a matter of logic, we should not expect to know anything with the same authority from any other source. But if Jesus does not speak from the perspective from which the whole content of History is known, then all this is worse than useless: it is simply making mischief with the teaching of the teachers of Israel.

A Sign for Falling and Rising.

Finally, Jesus Himself is a sign. In fact, He is *The Sign.* " The men of Ninevah ... repented at the preaching of Jonah, and behold a greater than Jonah is here .... [The Queen of Sheba] came from the ends of the earth to hear the wisdom of Solomon, and behold, something greater than Solomon is here" (*Mt* 12:41-42.) Both Jonah and the Queen of the south and all the signs that are bound up on their stories all point to this moment, as Jesus speaks now to the Pharisees. And so, both Jonah and the Queen are signs in yet another sense: they are like sign-posts, pointing, then and now, to Jesus, the Sign of signs.

We find Jesus designated as a sign early in the Gospels. In Luke's account, Jesus' birth is announced to the shepherds: " For to you is born this day in the city of David a Savior, who is Christ the Lord. And this will be a sign to you: you will find a babe wrapped in swaddling cloths, and lying in a manger "(*Lk* 2:11-12.) Luke also tells the story of the presentation of Jesus as the first-born child of Mary in the Temple at Jerusalem, where there was a man named Simeon:

> ... and this man was righteous and devout, looking for the consolation of Israel, and the Holy Spirit was upon him. And it had been revealed to him by the Holy Spirit that he should not see death before he had seen the Lord's Christ. And inspired by the Spirit he came into the temple; and when the parents brought in the child Jesus, to do for him according to the custom of the law, he took him up in his arms and blessed God and said, Lord, now lettest thou thy servant depart in peace, according to thy word; for mine eyes have seen thy salvation which thou has prepared in the presence of all peoples, a light for revelation to the Gentiles, and for glory to thy people Israel.
> And his father and his mother marveled at what was said about him; and Simeon blessed them and said to Mary his mother, Behold, this child is set for the fall and rising of many in Israel, and for a sign that is spoken against (and a sword will pierce through your own soul also), that thoughts out of many hearts may be revealed (*Lk* 2:25-35.)

The day following Jesus' entry into Jerusalem, when the crowds had shouted, "Hosanna! Blessed be he who comes in the name of the Lord! Blessed be the kingdom of our father David that is coming! Hosanna in the highest!" (*Mk* 11:9-10), Jesus and the disciples were returning from Bethany where they had spent the night, and "he was hungry. And seeing in the distance a fig tree in leaf, he went to see if he could find anything on it. When he came to it, he found nothing but leaves, for it was not the season [*kairos*] (11:13) for figs. And he said to it, 'May no one ever eat fruit from you again,' And his disciples heard it" (*Mk* 11:12-14.) In verses 15-19, Mark then tells the story of Jesus' driving the money-changers out of "my house." Then, "As they passed by in the [next] morning, they saw the fig tree withered away to its roots. And Peter [who is Mark's source for this eyewitness story] remembered and said to him, 'Master, look! The fig tree which you cursed has withered' " (*Mk* 11:20-21.)

At the time, what impressed the disciples about this incident was Jesus' power in causing the tree to wither by His word alone, illustrating yet again His apparently sovereign authority over nature. And in truth Jesus does make the incident an occasion for teaching on this point: "And Jesus answered them, 'Have faith in God. Truly, I say to you, whoever says to this mountain, "Be taken up and cast into the sea," and does not doubt in his heart, and believes that what he says will come to pass, it will be done for him. Therefore I tell you, whatever you ask in prayer, believe that you receive it, and you will' " (Mk 11:22-23.) It is relevant to our present theme to note that "this mountain"is not any old mountain. Most of the mountains that figure in a major way in the Bible, beginning with Sinai, and in the New Testament including the "high mountain" of Temptation (*Lk* 4:5), the Mount of Beatitudes (*Mt* 5:1), the Mount of Tansfiguration (*Mt* 17:1, *Mk* 9:2, *Lk* 9:28), are impossible to locate with absolute confidence today. But there is no doubt about the location of "this mountain." It is the Mount of Olives, or Olivet; of which the Prophet Zechariah predicted that, when the LORD has gathered all the nations to fight against Jerusalem, "Then the LORD will go forth and fight against those nations ... And in that day His feet will stand on the Mount of Olives, which faces Jerusalem on the east, and the Mount of Olives shall be split in two from east to west, making a very large valley ... then you shall flee through my mountain valley ... [etc.]" (*Zechariah* 14:3-5. [NKJV]). Here, Jesus confirms the prophecy that in the End of Time, this mountain will be removed.

Jesus, as we have already seen, frequently claimed and exercised the right to command obedience from Nature. This claim was the practical face of His claim to identity in substance with the Father. Here, Jesus has given no command to the tree; but He is angry to find that it is without fruit, despite the fact that it was not the season for fruit (*Mk* 11:13). This aspect of the story - the "irrationality" of Jesus' behaviour, the display of anger against a tree! -- troubles many people who have no difficulty about yet another nature-miracle. Several of Jesus' teachings, in these few days before His trial, turn on the dramatic and unexpected, even apparently bizarre, juxtaposition of the theme of season (*kairos*)-in-nature with the theme of season (*kairos*)-in- history. We must grasp, first of all, that these are not philosophical reflections. This is not Socrates, but Jesus. He is not ruminating on problems of meaning, from the outside, so to speak. He is not talking about ideas, but performing signs. He is telling them about divine presence and divine deeds. He is telling us the largest truths that there are to tell. They have to do with how Nature stands to History, and History to Nature - things that are known only from the perspective of eternity, where the full content of time is "seen" and (so to speak) studied.

All of what can be known about Nature is in principle (though never in fact) open to the human race as the fruit of all of our scientific strivings across the centuries. This is because the secrets of Nature are the recurring patterns within it: the same yesterday, today, and tomorrow. There is no reason, in principle, why we should not eventually hit upon all these patterns. But the secrets of History are not in principle open to our enquiry. For History is truth about sequences of singular events, whose patterns constantly change as new singular events are added over time. To be able to say anything with authority about History one would need the perspective from which the whole content of time is known - past, present and future.

The fig tree belongs to the first class of recurring symbols in Old Testament prophecy, usually, though not always, in association with the vine. It speaks of peace and contentment, of undisturbed domestic life - more specifically, of the peace and contentment of Israel, [14] and most notably in the context of Israel's ultimate victory over the last of her persecutors in the Messianic age. [15] The failure of the fig harvest amounts to doom. [16] These associations would occur immediately to Jesus' hearers. Jesus' quarrel with the fig tree would be seen as an acted-out parable, of the sort that Old Testament prophets were frequently put through - notably, Ezekiel in Chapters 3 through 5 of the Book of that prophet. These acted-out prophecies are embarrassing to read about. They make the point that God is willing to use all means to get His stubborn people to confront unpleasant messages that are necessary for their salvation. The people who were unmoved and even uninterested by Ezekiel's words, stop dead in their tracks to ask: What are you doing with those ropes? Why have you cut off your hair? Why are you dividing your hair into parcels of three? Why are you weighing out the three parcels? Jesus' quarrel with the fig tree is like one of Ezekiel's acted-out signs. What kind of a man would curse a fig tree for not bearing fruit when figs are out of season? The point of this ordinarily bizarre deed is to cause us to ask the question: What kind of a man ...? And the answer is: not one of a kind or type of man, but the One-of-a-kind, the One Who can command nature with the authority of its Creator.

Claiming to speak from the perspective where the whole content of history is known, Jesus says: we   are   further along   in the seasons of World History than anyone   here   can recognize.   The teachers of Israel and the people and   even the   disciples, in their different ways, have all failed   the test   of   seeing and responding to the signs   of   the   coming Kingdom.   Sooner than anyone guesses, there will   occur   the Sign   of signs, the Sign to which the sign of   Jonah points, the   open secret of the Old Testament: that the Son   of   Man must   die   at the hands of the Gentile   authorities   and   the Jews, then He must be hidden away for three days, and then He must   rise   again   from the dead.   This   is   the   work which completes   the   reconciliation   of man-to-man,   and   man-to-nature, and of man-and-nature-together to God.

The   tree   passively receives energies from   the   realm of natural forces acting around and within it.   It   has no   independent will.   It has no "sense of time".   It has   no "sense"   of anything.   Yet our text says that He   spoke   to it! (*Mk* 11:14).   He *blamed* it for not responding to His   own needs.   In   any of *us*, this behaviour would be bizarre.   And so   in   logic   it would be for anyone other than   He   Who   is identical in authority and in substance with its Creator.   The really powerful sign here is not the nature-miracle (the withering of the tree by His word), but the wonder   that Jesus addresses the tree! The key to all of this is that nature too is the object of   the Saviour's concern,   because   its   redemption is ultimately   to   follow   upon   the   redemption   of   man.   The redemption   of nature   is not His immediate   work;   but   its redemption is to be mediated through the redeemed *people*   who *are*   the immediate object of the Saviour's work.   Jesus sees the whole content of time, and He sees its conclusion in   the reinstatement   of the children of God in a   world   in   which nature too is redeemed - reconciled to man, and reconciled to God.

His   rebuke of all His human listeners   that   day   for their refusal to accept Him is mirrored in this rebuke   to the tree.   The   early Church   came   to   see   the story   of   its redemption   in this holistic context;   and then   the   otherwise embarrassing story of Jesus' rebuke of the fig tree came to be read for these meanings. Paul spelled out this teaching to the early Church in plain terms: "For the creation waits with eager longing for the revelation of the sons of God ... because the creation itself will be set free from its bondage to decay and obtain the glorious liberty of the children of God" (*Romans* 8:19 – 21.) In this light, we see Jesus' behaviour towards the fig tree as a sign, in the same category as "the sign of Jonah." Mankind's hostility towards God the Creator began with Adam, and its continuation has made impossible the exercise of His kingship over men in the human life-time of Jesus of Nazareth; and so long as it continues it will thwart the triumph of His Kingdom in the realm of History, until He comes again. Nature is at fault; but only because men are at fault - and Nature will continue to be at fault, until "our adoption as sons, the redemption of our bodies" (*Romans* 8:23.)

The final purpose that the Creator has for nature none of us can visualize. But in scripture we are told this much about it: that ultimately it will be utterly reconciled to man, and man-and-nature-together will be reconciled to God. Jesus claims to be the accomplisher of this New Creation - the Rod from the stem of Jesse, of *Isaiah* 11. When His work is done, "The wolf shall dwell with the lamb, and the leopard shall lie down with the kid, and the calf and the lion and the fatling together, and a little child shall lead them. The cow and bear shall feed; their young shall lie down together; and the lion shall eat straw like the ox. The suckling child shall play over the hole of the asp. And the weaned child shall put his hand on the adder's den. They shall not hurt or destroy in all my holy mountain; for the earth shall be full of the knowledge of the LORD as the waters cover the sea" (*Isaiah* 11:6-9.) Jesus claims to see all of this now, as they walk the road from Bethany to Jerusalem, and He turns to speak to a fig tree! Now, speaking from the perspective of eternity, where His life is complete and His death is complete and His resurrection is complete,

He judges the fig tree for toiling on under the limitations of the old creation, just as he judged His disciples for toiling on under the limitations of the old creation when confronted with cases that needed healing (e.g., *Mt* 17:14-21.)

Finally, taking the whole story of Jesus' cursing of the fig tree as a sign in the largest sense, it points to Him, the Sign of signs. It is a sign for falling and rising. It presents us with a test: to follow it, or not to follow it. We cannot grasp everything that is being said here. But then, we can never expect to grasp, truly to appropriate, any truth of the first rank of importance. But something like this is at its heart: that henceforth we are not to live in time as though the processes of Nature, on which our natural life depends, are the measure of our singular meaning; because now we know, with the authority of the Creator, that these processes, taken together, are to be understood as sub-processes of the governing process in reality - which is the Sacred History, the work of Redemption which Jesus of Nazareth now sees, in this moment of His encounter with the fig tree, completed.

Chapter Four: The Scandal of End Times.

"The Pornography of Faith."

Some years ago, I was approached for advice by a student who was preparing to write for another professor (in the Political Science Department) a paper on the theme, "Millennialism as a Factor in Contemporary American Politics." He wanted some leads on the most influential millennialist literature of the 1970's and '80's. There was no need to reflect on this: I knew that no less an authority than the *New York Times* had reported that the largest-selling non-fiction book for the entire decade of the 1970's was Hal Lindsey's, *The Late, Great Planet Earth* (1970.) [1] But the book, we then discovered, was not on the shelves of our University's Library! So we jointly requested that the library purchase a copy.

To make a long and painful story short, it took me a full year of lobbying and protesting to get that ten-dollar book into the permanent collection of the Library. The matter had to be fought through two levels of University committees, and eventually involved Deans, Chairmen, and the Vice-President of the University. Initial opposition came from the Library's Purchaser of Books in Religion who reported that, "having had the chance to examine it ... [I find that my] misgivings prove justified, and I am more than ever of the opinion that the book has no place in an academic library. (I am not speaking of the subject-matter so much as the manner of presentation.)" The University Librarian upheld this judgement: "The reason is not that I wish to impose any form of censorship on the selection of materials for the collection, nor that I and [the Purchaser] do not approve of the book. We do not think that it is a suitable book for permanent retention in the collection." The Purchaser, "wondering whether I was being too fastidious," then sought support for her judgement by consulting computer information on Canadian library holdings, and found only five University Libraries that hold the book. This last point is worth registering, lest it be thought that my University's attitude is untypical, and that in bringing this story into the pages of this book I have lost the proper perspective. This determination not to be out of line with the most respectable opinion on these matters seemed to be a feature in the behaviour of everyone I dealt with in that year of hassling for shelf-space for *The Late, Great Planet Earth*. The mildest version of this concern was in the memo with which, at the end of the struggle, the Chairman of the Senate Committee on the University Library announced to me the narrow verdict in favour of overriding the Purchaser and the librarian: "The Committee believed ... that the book's particular religious orientation was such as to open the possibility of misjudgement, and that in such cases the wisest policy is to err on the side of inclusion rather than that of exclusion."

Why is there this solicitude about the "possibility of misjudgement" in the field of Christian eschatology when the University has abandoned its role *in loco parentis* on every other front: moral, philosophical and aesthetic? Given the universally-conceded fact of the book's impact on the mind of this generation, why should we make this exception to our proudly trumpeted "openness", our devotion to "free enquiry"? Why do we make it here, and not somewhere else? Why are the possibilities of "misjudgement" so horrifying here, when we take them in stride with regard to everything else that comes off the presses? How can a University, which thinks of itself as holding up the light of free enquiry to the whole world, entertain even for a moment the thought of getting along without a single copy of the one book that was most widely-read by the whole population it is pretending to study and to lead?

This case illustrates a general truth about the world of learning and the world of opinion-making which depends on it. There is an unshakable determination in the house of liberal learning (so-called) to deny the persistence of vital religious faith in real life. The notion that learned minds must acquaint themselves in even minimal ways with what is really in the minds of the masses of the people about whom they so freely deliver their "scientific", "disinterested", "objective" judgements, cannot occur in the academic milieu today. University Departments of Sociology teach in lock-step fashion that Religion is withering away under the effects of universal public education. Nonetheless, Karl Marx, Emile Durkheim and Max Weber, who were the principal suppliers of the vocabulary that is supposed to describe this process, were wrong. Not partially wrong, or sort-of-wrong, but totally wrong. It is not merely that the secularization of which they spoke has not been completed. It never began.

Today, more than ever, the masses of Americans (whether for good or ill is not the present point) think in religious categories when they think of the largest purposes which History is unfolding. Opinion polls bear this out consistently. [2] Most people see their nation and other nations as instruments of large and eternal purposes, figures involved in a Plan, the largest features of which they feel they know confidently because the Bible gives us an outline of them. Whether any of this commends itself to the individual who happens to be the researcher ought to be beside the point - the point, that is, of his being a researcher, a scholar. We have several copies of *Mein Kampf* in our University Library. And so we should. Nobody I know personally makes any case for the historical or philosophical learning to be found there. But equally no one pretends that we can know the mind of Germany past or present, without it. We do not have to have an opinion whether its message was for good or ill in order to know that we must take it into account. This is surely inarguable. But *The Late, Great Planet Earth* strikes fear into the heart of the liberal academic, as *Mein Kampf* does not. And this is not because the latter is a book from the past, whose influence is done. Indeed, there are still some people who read *Mein Kampf* intending to be persuaded by it; and some of them are, and thereby lose their souls. But this appalling truth does not constitute a reason for excluding it from University Libraries; indeed, it is among the reasons for including it. No defender of liberal learning (as truly defined) would deny this.

Why does Christian "eschatalogical" literature evoke contempt so extreme that academic scholarship will not even look at it, and will not, unless virtually forced by an eccentric and persistent senior faculty member, to house any part of it in its libraries, lest *any of us* look at it either? We have seen already that scholarship cannot deny its "significance" - that is, its real overwhelming popular impact - which, in a democracy, is supposed to count for something. But there, I believe, is the real sticking-point. It is precisely because of its enormous public impact that it must be excluded from the shelves.

It is crucial, furthermore, to note that the line here does not run between the atheists and the theists. Rather, the line runs between the learned mind and the popular mind; for a powerful and telling feature of the contemporary story of suppression of the literature of eschatology is that the most vigorous censors of this literature are the learned theologians.

"Ratlos vor der Apokalyptik."

The liberal churchman's terror in the presence of "eschatology" is brilliantly caught and rightly named in John Updike's novel, *A Month Of Sundays* (1974). Updike tells the story of a successful clergyman of one of the mainline denomination who has been caught out by his wife and his Board in a nettle of adulterous liaisons. It is agreed by his Board that he should go off to a desert facility in the Southwest which is especially set aside for clergymen in need of psychiatric help. Towards the end of the book, as it is beginning to appear that the opportunity for reflection has done our hero some of the good intended, we find the clergymen-patients on a recreational outing to a park. As they walk from the bus through the parking-lot, they are confronted by a young man, who interrupts the therapeutic occasion by thrusting at them pamphlets of "cretinous prophecy ... produced in Dallas and repulsive in its crazed computations and slangy piety." Illustrated "with cartoons of Richard Nixon collapsed beneath a 'Shield of Incredibility' and with intricate diagrams of the Sun's perihelion and the comet Kahoutek's orbit in relation to the November ceasefire and the Winter equinox ... [it] predicts the end of the world in eighty days." [3] The clergy fall back in panicky horror. All the hours of therapeutic counselling have been undone in an instant!

In the days before this crisis, the hero has, as it happens, been reading the fifteenth chapter of Paul's *First Letter to the Corinthians*. He has been writing (for his own eyes only) a sermon on the text, "And if Christ be not risen, then is our preaching vain, and your faith also in vain."

> Paul expected it to happen soon: "Behold, I show you a mystery: we shall not all sleep, but we shall all be changed, in a moment, in the twinkling of an eye, at the last trump" ... Yet still men listen for that last trump. ... [B]ut let us ask ourselves, is not the content of this miserable throwaway [the "cretinous prophecy" in the

pamphlet] promulgated by the most desperate inanity of a desperately inane generation, is not the content, as distinct from the style, the content of our life's call, and our heart's deepest pledge? .... Is not our distaste here aesthetic, where aesthetics are an infernal category; is not our love of Christianity an antiquarian and elitist cherishing, a dark and arcane swank, where a living faith for the lowly should obtain? Does not this pornography of faith, like the pornography of copulation printed in the same grimy shop, testify to a needed miracle, a true wonder, a miraculous raw truth which it is one of civilization's conspiracies to suppress? ... Is not the situation in our churches indeed that from the pulpit we with our good will and wordy humanism lean out to tempt our poor sheep from these scraps of barbaric doctrine, preserved in the creed like iguanodon footprints in limestone, that alone propel them out from their pleasant beds on a Sunday morning? [4]

Updike's clergyman, unlike, perhaps, some of the atheist objectors, knows that these "scraps of barbaric doctrine" which have inspired the young pamphleteer to his freelance publication, do belong to the creed: "... He ascended into heaven, and sits at the right hand of the Father, from thence he shall come to judge the quick and the dead ..." He knows, therefore, that the violence of his flight from the extreme and unschooled speculations which the young man is offering gives away the awareness within himself of betrayal. *He is a civilized man, before he is a believer in the supernatural.* And he knows that the "distaste" for these doctrines among learned clergy is so absolute because they have come to believe that their welfare depends on their being able to talk to learned non-Christians in the language of the learned post-Christian culture. For sanity's sake, these barbaric doctrines must be kept out of view.

Civilized Christians, both clerical and lay, find confirmation for their antipathy towards eschatology in the house of academic theology, where eschatology is handled as plain pornography. Logically enough, there is very little academic literature on this theme. Exceptions are: Klaus Koch. *The*

Re-Discovery of the Apocalyptic (1972), and John J. Collins, *The Apocalyptic Imaginiation* (1987.) (See "Bibliographical Essay.") Klaus Koch sums up the story of Nineteenth and early-Twentieth Century continental theology when he says that "Apocalyptic literature had never played any part in university courses in theology. Even today it is nowhere an examination subject." [5] John J. Collins wrote *The Apocalyptic Imagination* (1987) to show that in the life of the early Church there was an inextricable connection between faith in the gospel and faith in the eschatological expectations that we find in what is called the "apocalyptic" literature of that age. Collins begins his book by noting and endorsing a judgement of Ernst Kasemann: that "apocalyptic was the mother of all Christian theology." [6] If this is so, there is no possibility of our accepting or rejecting the Gospel which the first witnesses declared unless we at least hear out what they preached about "End Times." Yet, Collins notes, "the primary apocalyptic texts have received only sporadic attention and are often avoided or ignored by Biblical scholarship." From Klaus Koch, Collins borrows the original German to speak of the theologians' "*Ratlos vor der Apokalyptic*"". (The word *Rat* is from a root that means something like "having a supply" or a "stock". So *Ratlos* is "without supply" or "without resources" - hence, "unable to deal with," or "unable to handle." Collins translates, "embarrassed by apocalyptic.")

> The great academic authorities of the Nineteenth Century, such as Julius Wellhausen and Emil Schurer, slighted its value, considering it to be a product of "Late Judaism" which was greatly inferior to the prophets; and this attitude is still widespread today ... Whatever we may decide about the theological value of these writings, it is obvious that a strong theological prejudice can impede the task of historical reconstruction and make it difficult to pay enough attention to the literature to enable us to understand it at all. It will be well to reserve theological judgement until we have mastered the literature. [7]

That last point seems obvious enough to any outsider to the guild of academic theologians: namely, that (to paraphrase Collins) scholars should pay enough attention to a certain literature to be able to understand it before making judgements about it! There is a great gap on the shelves that hold the academic literature of theology, and a correspondingly great absence in their textbooks, where there ought to be lively, serious, and learned discussion of what is called in the Hebrew Bible "the Day of the Lord", or just "That Day" - what the early Church called the *parousia* (the Appearing of Christ at the End) - what the popular literature of today calls End Times. Theologians, who have to live in the world of liberal learning, are most reluctant to admit that such material played a formative role in early Christianity, because they know that in most minds the word "apocalyptic" is associated with fanatical millennarian expectation.

In the English-speaking world, eschatological speculation has always been identified with disorderly popular forces. Given the toleration of religious dissent in the Anglo/American tradition, these forces could not be contained by the Church establishment, as they could on the continent. Eschatological literature in the English world, and particularly in the United States, is, therefore, almost entirely *popular* literature. In the United States, the disestablishment of the original state churches (Congregational in New England, Anglican elsewhere) was followed by the Great Revival, and thereafter by recurring evangelical revivals which spawned new "denominations", new and less "learned" seminaries and Bible Schools, and popular religious presses, to which would be drawn most of the authors of End Times books and pamphlets. In the U.S.A., popular religion has a social significance and a political strength that it has nowhere else. Non-affiliated "religious publishers" thrive by challenging the credibility and the market share of the Church-related presses and the academic presses, which publish the works of the learned clergy;

and this they do by publishing what the learned presses will not. Updike's hero supposes that "the cretinous pamphlet" will have been published in Dallas. Possibly so. Certainly, it will not have been published in Boston.

The Politics of Kingdom-Theology.

There is a powerful political dimension to this matter - taking the word "politics" in the fullest sense, as bearing on the whole possibility of exercising influence in all of the places where real *power* is wielded, including the realm of education and information (the media), as well as the realm of public authority. The repudiation of *apocalyptic literature* by academic scholarship, and consequently by preachers and teachers who look to academic scholarship, took place coincidentally with and in response to the secularization of learning in the Universities. By rapid stages beginning in the early Nineteenth Century, it became clear to learned theologians that the continuation of their lease within the house of academic learning depended upon maintaining the "credibility" of theological arguments - that is, maintaining some form of exchangeability between the currency of God-talk and the currency of secular learning. This could only be achieved by abandoning the specific vocabulary of dogmatic theology. At the same time, and hand-in-hand with this, forces were at work (beginning early in the Nineteenth Century in continental Europe, somewhat later in Great Britain, somewhat later still in North America) that were reducing the place of discussion of God and God's purposes in the political realm, culminating, by mid-Twentieth Century (in the case of the United States) in the complete eradication of theological references from the theater of public discussion. Clergy who wish to maintain some place for themselves in the realm of political discussion have simply abandoned the specific vocabulary of dogmatic theology.

This is too immense a topic for us here. Our present purpose is specifically to suggest how this process of secularization led to disparagement of eschatology among the theologians. If we look back to the opening years of the Twentieth Century, we find the Protestant clergy of the United States still playing a leading role in the setting of the political agenda of what is called the Progressive Era.. Those were the days of "Social Gospel." While it was no longer customary (as it had been in the beginning of the story, in Puritan times) to rehearse the dogmatic content of the Christian faith in public settings, there were still in those days occasions generally agreed to be appropriate for explicitly addressing in public the God of the Christian faith, the generally acknowledged source of national and cultural values. For the last time ever, the politicians of this age used (selectively) the vocabulary of received Christian theology in the broad light of day. As late as the opening year of the Great War, there was, in Henry May's words, a "national faith" and, in the broad light of day, everybody owned it. Indeed, "the most effective preachers of the national faith in this period ... were not ministers but statesmen." [8] Consider the case of Theodore Roosevelt, who stood before the Long Island Bible Society of his own community of Oyster Bay and declared, "If we read the Bible aright, we read a book which teaches us to go forth and do the work of the Lord. That work can be done only by the man who is neither a weakling nor a coward, by the man who in the fullest sense of the word is a Christian." [9] By the 1930s, such talk would be denounced by the entire constituency of political commentators as a violation of the "Wall of Separation" which shelters public life from theology. In the Progressive Era, politicians took for granted that sound politics stood upon sound (that is "progressive") theology. When an adversary went awry, it was because his theology was awry; in such dangerous cases it was necessary to bring this to light. Thus, an editorial from the *Outlook*, a journal edited by

Lyman Abbott and Theodore Roosevelt, puts the 1912 Presidential contest between Woodrow Wilson and Theodore Roosevelt himself into theological context:

> The Democratic Party appeals to those who are dissatisfied with present conditions and desire to return to the conditions of a previous age. They look to the past for their ideal; they wish to return to the simplicity of the fathers. They are men who in their theology go back for their beliefs to the creeds of the sixteenth century, or even to those of the fourth, and regard all new doctrines as heresies ... We look forward, not backward, to the Golden Age. We believe in a new theology, a new science, a new sociology, a new politics. We believe that in every day walks a better tomorrow; the world is steadily growing better, though with lapses, failures and retrogressions. We believe ... that the twentieth century is as competent to make its theological creed as was the sixteenth or fourth. [10]

Walter Rauschenbusch caught the spirit of Social Gospel better than anyone else: "Humanity is waiting for a revolutionary Christianity which will call the old world evil and change it ... The essential purpose of Christianity was to transform human society into the Kingdom of God ... The largest and hardest part of the work of Christianizing the social order has been done." [11]

It soon became clear, however, that people who said these things did not correctly appraise up the world in which they were living, on the eve of the War that marked the beginning of the ruin of Western civilization. Moreover, it was false in its spirit: they were using words in ways that falsified their real meanings. They had betrayed the legacy of dogmatic theology by bartering away its specific vocabulary in exchange for vocabulary borrowed from the repertoire of liberal philosophy. "Christian" now meant "civilized" or "of good will." "God" now meant "process." The "Kingdom of God" now meant a perfectly- redesigned political community.

America was, however, no longer a "biblical commonwealth." More to the point: not even the clergy would claim that their prescriptions for the good society derived from the Bible. James M. Whiton, the editor of an influential series of "Works on Modern Theology" spoke for the majority of liberal clergy when he said: "That the systematic theology framed by 'the old divines' has hopelessly broken down in the collapse of the ancient conceptions of God, of Nature, of the Bible, and of man, which molded and sustained it, is now frankly confessed in the chief seats of theological instruction." [12]

Social Gospel self-confidence was based on a totally false impression that the mind and the heart of the American nation were Christian. Compounding the possibilities of "false consciousness" (as the Marxists say) that would follow from *that* error were those that follow from another equally false but "fundamental idea": that the message of the gospel and the message of secular wisdom of the Nineteenth Century were complementary aspects of "a unity of reality."

Prior to the Nineteenth Century, it would have been assumed by theologians that a responsible doctrine of the Kingdom of God should begin with what Jesus said. As Christ used the term - "The Kingdom," or "the Kingdom of God," or "the Kingdom of Heaven" - it expressed the final and inclusive Purpose which God has for mankind and for creation. The fact was that the liberals' attitude of sovereign liberty with respect to the authority of the Bible and the historic creeds precluded any possibility of a responsible doctrine of the Kingdom. For ambitious social gospelers, the Kingdom was a free-floating concept, capable of taking up any statement of program from whatever source that speaks of an ideal relation of man to man or of man to nature. This can be tested simply. One need only substitute the phrase, "a better future," for the phrase, "Kingdom of God," in any statement taken from Rauschenbusch's corpus or that of his emulators, and one will quickly see that in every case it works - that is, it captures, without the need for addition or subtraction, the whole thought of the original.

The Social Gospel preachers liked to picture themselves as Old Testament prophets - as, incidentally, do the Liberation theologians of today. They liked to quote, and to attach themselves to, the classical prophets' thunderings against the rich, the priests, incense, luxury, and fatted calves. They *rightly* linked Jesus to this tradition of prophetic protest against injustice and false worship. Alertness to the radical social message of the Old Testament prophets was not the thing that separated the liberal theologians from the conservative theologians, then or now. Social Gospelers, however, unlike the theological conservatives, refused to acknowledge that part of the message of both Jesus and the prophets that spoke of the Kingdom *in apocalyptic terms* - that is, as appearing suddenly, in God's time, to sweep away the present order of things in the cosmos, and to replace all with "*new heavens and a new earth*". "Translate," said Rauschenbusch, "the evolutionary theories into religious faith, and you have the doctrine of the Kingdom of God. This combination with scientific evolutionary thought has freed the Kingdom ideal of its catastrophic setting and its background of demonism, and so adapted it to the climate of the modern world." [13] Social Gospelers simply denied that Jesus had any interest in the eschatological ideas that figure in the Jewish tradition. Francis Peabody, for example, explained that when Jesus spoke of the Kingdom coming as a seed growing or leaven working, he must be understood "above the heads of his reporters." What He really had in mind was "evolution (although he could scarcely have been expected to use that word [*sic*!], and his use of biological analogies indicates that he presupposed an organic society." [14]

In this confidence that they can raise the materialistic or superstitious imagery of the Gospel to a *higher* key, the Social Gospelers are at one with the Liberation theologians of today. Unlike the Liberation theologians, for whom the vocabulary of *revolution* is the hidden heart of the Gospel, the Social Gospel theologians prided themselves on their irenic spirit. On its reverse side of this irenism is a greedy assimilationism - a buoyant confidence that all "progressive forces" were engaged on the one great path to the one great truth, presently best expressed by themselves. There is one place, and one place only, where their irenic spirit fails them, however. This is on the matter of "eschatology."

The eminent Social Gospel teacher Shirley Jackson Case of the University of Chicago published an article on "The Premillenial Menace" in *Biblical World*, then followed it up with a book, The *Millenial Hope: A Phase of Wartime Thinking*. Both appeared in 1918, and both were products of haste and spleen. "The American nation," Case observed in 1918, "is engaged in a gigantic effort to make the world safe for democracy ... Under ordinary circumstances one might excusably pass over premillennarianism as a wild and relatively harmless fancy. But in the present time of testing it would be almost traitorous negligence to ignore the detrimental character of the premillennial propaganda. By proclaiming that wars cannot be eliminated until Christ returns and that in the meantime the world must grow constantly worse, this type of teaching strikes at the very root of our present national endeavor to bring about a new day for humanity, when this old earth shall be made a better place in which to live, and a new democracy of nations shall arise to render wars impossible ... Premillennialists resent the suggestion that enemy gold is behind their activities, and one group of them has publicly affirmed that the federal authorities' inspection of their books failed to justify this suspicion. However that may be, we have in the premillennial propaganda as a whole an instance of serious economic waste by which large sums of money are being diverted from projects that might contribute directly to the success of the war."[15] This is precisely the thinking and the spirit that would in a latter context be called "McCarthyism."

Social Gospelers were certain that the apocalyptic hope had never figured at all in the message of the classical Old Testament prophets. They rested their case upon the brilliant dodge accomplished by the Wellhausian form-critics: according to this, all talk of Last Things emerged in later, less healthy, times long after the classical prophets had gone, when the well of true prophecy had run dry, when the essentially desperate and escapist notion of "a new heaven and a new earth" had replaced the visions of human community restored by human effort. Likewise, liberal historical scholarship on the New Testament followed the lead of David F. Strauss (1808-74) in separating "the historical Jesus" from all words and sayings that appeared to endorse apocalyptic views. Going "above the heads of his reporters," they could see that He either did not say the things the Gospels present Him as saying, or that He was winking at Nineteenth Century liberal scholars as He did. The problematics of textual criticism and historical questions were never rehearsed by the Social Gospel theologians in any of their widely-read books. All of that was presumed to have been done by the giants of Old Testament and New Testament who had laboured over the past threee generations. It was simply stated that these are "the commonplaces of scientific biblical study." Take it or leave it.

An entirely unlooked-for complication for the world-view of Protestant liberals arose contemporaneously with the appearance of the principal books of Social Gospel theology, when Albert Schweitzer proposed, in the very name of scientific-historical criticism, that Jesus' own message was through-and-through "eschatological." Indeed, Schweitzer argued that the passages of the Gospels most thoroughly eschatological in character were precisely those most surely to be assigned to Him! [16] This threat to settled liberal views from the side of German scholarship so enraged the usually benign Walter Rauschenbusch that he fired off this piece of rather ignorant calumny:

My own conviction is that the professional theologians of Europe, who all belong by kinship and sympathy to the bourgeois classes and are constitutionally incapacitated for understanding any revolutionary ideas, past or present, have overemphasized the ascetic and eschatological elements in the teachings of Jesus. They have classed as ascetic or eschatological apocalyptic the radical sayings about property and non-resistance which seem to them impractical or visionary. If the present chastisement of God [i.e., the War] purges our intellects of capitalistic and upper-class iniquities we shall no longer damn these sayings of Jesus by calling them eschatological, but shall exhibit them as anticipations of the fraternal ethics of democracy and prophecies of common sense.[17]

Notice that Rauschenbusch makes no attempt to meet the learned thesis with a learned argument. He was, of course, out of his league in these technical-scholarly matters. Instead, he simply crushes a learned argument with political slogans -- and puerile slogans at that. (Could there be anything sillier than the notion of Albert Schweitzer as the toady of capitalist bosses?) It is interesting to compare this outburst with the consistently deferential posture that Rauschenbusch had assumed towards pre-War German "scientific-historical" scholarship, so long as it sustained the liberal image of the Christ of the social prophets.

What is behind these violent outbursts against any and all versions of the apocalyptic hope? Social Gospelers were painfully aware that questions about End Times were increasingly occupying their laity, and this deeply alarmed them. At root, their fear was that the church would lose its credibility in enlightened company. They rightly saw that their present prestige as spokesmen for the age was bound up with their promotion of a convergence of the Kingdom-hope of Christian faith with the secular vision of progress towards the New Man. When presented with a clear choice between the alien world-view of the Gospels (its "catastrophic setting," its "background of demonism") and the modern world view, Social Gospelers did not hesitate: "Today religious fancy must submit to the factual restraints of scientific sanity." [18] During the War years, a mountain of End Times books and pamphlets poured forth from obscure presses. This phenomenon exposed the nightmare-truth that the restless and truculent laity did not believe in the convergence of the Christian vision of the Kingdom with the secular vision of progress. There was no squaring that circle. Social Gospelers had won their place in the seats of learning and of politics by their claim to be able to harness the best elements of the Church to the work of realizing the Kingdom of God ("A Better Future") on this earth. In once-born faith, there is no place for any Second Coming.

*   *   *

The vehemence of the liberals' denunciation of the millennialists is the best clue to their desperate determination not to accept the true - that is, the *subcultural*, standing of Christian faith and doctrine. The contempt for "eschatology" which was so crucial to the self- understanding and self-esteem of Protestant leaders in the Progressive era has not declined, but may even have intensified - if that seems possible. But the *political* setting is quite different. There is no longer any institutional presence of the Church in public life. Instead, there is the "Naked Public Square" described by Richard J. Neuhaus. The liberal clergy have not abandoned their political ambition - which is, to be acknowledged as the voice of the nation's conscience. But politicians are no longer giving them encouragement; or, for that matter, the time of day. Long ago, the politicians stopped playing the game of sprinkling their rhetoric with theological references. They will not stand on platforms with clergymen while prayers are given. This goes not only for "political" events, but for any and all public occasions, including graduation ceremonies, the cutting of ribbons for shopping-center openings, and so on. Prayers or any other form of

"God-talk" have gone from all public occasions - not so much because legal decisions have chased them away, as because the politicians are now simply embarrassed, and the public does not expect it anymore.

Meanwhile, there has been a steady migration of mainstream theological teaching and learning out of the denominational seminaries, once responsible for maintaining some degree of accountability to the historic creeds and the confessions of the particular churches (Presbyterian, Lutheran, Roman Catholic, whatever), and into University Departments of Religion and Graduate Schools of Theology. The sense of theology's accountability to secular learning has been greatly intensified since the Progressive days, when already "Fundamentalists" were charging that accountability to the creeds had been forfeited by the intellectuals. Now more than ever, the academic theologians distance themselves from popular, unlearned religious literature, the literature of the uncertified. To head off the possibility of being associated with the mind-set of Fundamentalism, the liberal clergy have put themselves at the head of the posse against the End Times pamphleteers. Given that there is virtually no contemporary learned (that is, academic) literature on the theme, the shelf of the library where the label "Eschatology" used to be is now bare. This abandonment of eschatology amounts to willful betrayal of a crucial section of dogmatic faith - the section which speaks of Christ's "return to judge the quick and the dead." The academic theologians have put forth few reasons for their avoidance of eschatology; and most of wht passes for reason is evasion. Most academic theologians simply deny the relevance to Modern Man of "eschatological" themes. They have sought to scare the learned and the semi-learned away with warnings that good minds go strange when they get down on all fours with the themes that fascinate the unlearned authors of popular eschatology.

So we have a vicious circle: the scholars having abandoned the themes of eschatology, declare the ground to be barren because there is no scholarship there! The gifts of mind that we rightly associate with the best of formal learning - deliberateness of method, patient restraint in the face of difficult and contradictory evidence, civility in the expression of differences, tolerance of a variety of methods - all these gifts have been chased from the field of eschatology.

As John Updike's vignette declares, there is treason at the heart of this fastidiousness. Academic scholars have no right to their swaggering contempt for the pamphleteers. It is because the learned have defected from the field, in fear of its well- known traps and mines, that the unlearned and reckless so nearly monopolize it. The academic scholars have not met the popular authors (the Lindseys, the de Haans, the Jack Van Impes, and the others) on level ground. Tendentious and sometimes ludicrous "Source" theories have simply bulldozed the field. "Predictive" prophecy has been categorically denounced as fraud - sometimes (but not always) conceded to be "pious" fraud. Theological students are told that what is presented in Scripture as prospective knowledge is in reality retrospective knowledge: *vaticinium ex eventu*. Of this, much more later.

But let us suppose that all of the arguments which liberal scholars have used against the possibility of predictive prophecy are sound and irreproachable; and let us suppose that all the various historical, cultural-anthropological, linguistic, sociological, and psychological theories which underlie the academics' rejections of prophecy are all in agreement with each other (which, of course, they are not); and suppose further that all of the "conservative" (i.e., creedal) scholarship that denounces the historical, cultural-anthropological, linguistic, sociological, and psychological theories of the liberals is all irredeemably wrong - should not the liberals *nonetheless* be speaking out for the right of this side to be heard, to display its wrong theories and evidence in the learned market?

Of course they should.

But of course they do not.

And here is the deepest treason of all. The Departments of Religion stand shoulder-to-shoulder with the University Librarians and Purchasers of Books. Their lock-step attitudes freeze eschatological literature out of the book review sections of their journals. As the expert readers of the manuscripts proposed to book-publishers, they are in position to warn the latter against the risks of putting their distinguished names and colophons on "unscholarly" or "popularizing" works. In fact, the atheist can be a far better ally in making the conservative theologians's case against censorious librarians than the scholars of Religion. The atheist has heard from his colleagues in the Religion Department that such books are of low scholarly merit and expose the anti-intellectual effects of popular religion. Cunning atheists do not hesitate to ecourage this result by escorting these books to the library's shelf! As Updike's clergyman confesses to himself: the theologian hates this literature precisely because in the moral sense it *does* belong to him. It *is* irrational, precisely as the atheist claim. And the very last thing the University's accredited spokesmen for Religion need is to be classified as "irrational."

The Case of Isaac Newton: "Shady Lucubrations" At the Dawn of Modern Science.

There was a time when reflection on "End Times" was a proud feature of the general, mainstream intellectual enterprise of our civilization; when, indeed, it occupied some of the best energies of some of our most famous ntellectuals. Hearing this, the reader's mind will probably flash back to the Middle Ages, perhaps the Tenth or Eleventh Century. But in fact I have in mind

the early Eighteenth Century.   This proved to be the last such moment, however;
and so the story deserves a little attention here.

Consider the reputation of Isaac Newton (1642-1727).

Every   reader will know that Isaac Newton founded the   modern
understanding (obtaining until recently) of the fundamental laws of behaviour of
physical bodies. His formulations made it possible to think of expressing all
relationships between all parts of everything that exists in the cosmos in
mathematical terms. Following the lead of Voltaire (not a scientist, but a
brilliant publicist), the generation of intellectuals who followed Newton spoke
of a "Newtonian" world-view and what it would mean to the future of mankind,
more-or-less as follows:

(i) that it made possible for the first time and for ever an absolutely clear
understanding of what was reasonable and hence of what was unreasonable;

(ii)   the reasonable being that which   is   objectively   knowable, because
reducible without remainder to mathematical (or geometric) definition - that
is, wholly describable in accurate terms of position in time and space, and thus
ultimately in *numbers*;

(iii) the unreasonable being everything else - that is, everything we think we
know, but cannot describe, without remainder, in numbers.

This mainstream-Enlightenment, Voltarian, view is what people have in mind
when they speak today of the Newtonian world-view. But that was not Newton's
vision of reality at all. [19] The notion that the whole of reality could be
explained, without remainder, in terms that described the relations between
physical bodies he rejected as blasphemous.   For Newton was, in truth, a
religious man - indeed a pious man, whose religious views were unabridgeably
supernaturalist. He was absolutely persuaded that this realm of our life in time

and space belongs to, or is perhaps a corner of, the realm of eternity. To understand how we mortals stand with respect to this realm of eternity, we need, he said, to learn an altogether different set of descriptive laws than those that he himself had built *for the description of the natural order alone* upon the fact of gravity. These larger laws, he believed, had been laid out in unambiguous terms *in Scripture*. They are the deep laws that govern World History; they are the principles which govern the visions of all the Prophets.

The laws that govern the unfolding of the Divine Plan of History are larger than the laws of gravity. The latter are (somehow) a subset of the former. Newton believed that "There were operational designs [in astronomy, mathematics, physics, and] in history ... [and these have] a similarly simple pattern - one so simple that it could be contained in two small books, Daniel and the Apocalypse, that were really repetitions of each other." [20] These views Newton worked out a great length in manuscripts to which he gave paractically the whole of his last years.

But in extreme contrast with Hal Lindsey in our own time, Newton was not seeking a popular audience for his eschatological speculations. He was very much an elitist. He believed that he belonged to an infinitesimally small rank of geniuses, going back to ancient Egyptian and Babylonian times, to whom had been vouchedsafe an extraordinary gift for uncovering the deep laws behind the appearances that everyone else wallows in. He believed it would do no good to invite the whole world to share the product of his lifelong research in Biblical prophecy. (This anti- democratic spirit, this inclination to esoteric visions, notions of secret brotherhoods of genius linking the contemporary erudite to seers of ancient times - this is all quite characteristic of Newton's time, with modern Freemasonry on the horizon.) An even larger matter for our consideration is that Newton's self-directed studies in theology and ancient literature had led him to very unorthodox theological conclusions. He became a "Socinian" - that is, an updated Arian, one who denies the Trinity. He went to great lengths to avoid theological discussion, though he spent his best energies (*literally* his best energies) reading and writing theology. (It should be recalled that to hold anti-Trinitarian views in England, even as late as the Eighteenth Century, closed all doors to scholarly careers; certainly, it would have closed the door to King's College, Cambridge, where Newton worked.) In his lifetime, only a fragment of Newton's theological composition was published with his authorization. Newton's literary heirs were shocked when, on his death, they opened the famous trunk to find the unmistakable evidence that the largest research project on which he had been involved throughout his life was not his work in Physics, Optics, Astronomy or Mathematics, but an exhaustive analysis of all the prophetic portions of the Old and New Testaments, concentrating especially on the Book of *Daniel* and the Apocalypse of St. John (that is, *Revelation.*) To accomplish this work, he had mastered the Biblical languages of Hebrew and Greek. By far the largest part of his library was made up of Biblical commentaries and theological works. "He became," says Frank Manuel, "a master of the traditional tools of scriptural exegesis as developed by the rabbis of the Talmud, Church Fathers, medieval commentators, and Protestant divines." [21]

It is important to note that this enthusiasm for Biblical study and for speculation on eschatological themes in particular was not considered eccentric in his time. We find that many of his own circle of intellectuals were involved in similar research and composition. Manuel describes "the huge number of books" of eschatological speculation which came from Newton's circle. He speaks of the effort of imagination that our contemporaries have to make to grasp the continued fascination of great European intellects of the seventeenth and early eighteenth centuries with the interpretation of Daniel and the

Apocalypse. In retrospect, we may see this as the swansong of learned research and publication in Biblical eschatology. "With the triumph of the philosophes, this type of literature, though it increased in quantity, became the refuge of cranks and an occasional poetic or artistic genius. In the seventeenth century it was still at the core of the religion of a scholarly divine" - and, as we have seen, of many a lay intellectual.

That not one in a thousand of us who have heard the doubtful story about the apple has ever heard anything about Newton's speculations on prophecy is a fact full of significance for the theme of this chapter: that is, the commitment of the world of learning to suppression of any and all evidence of the persistent allure of the supernatural, particularly as it reflects itself in enthusiasm for Biblical eschatology. That Newton was "a religious man" is generally conceded. And it is sometimes said that he made a contribution to the persistence of faith in God the Creator, in that his "system" retained some place for the interventions of an active God Who adjusts certain irregularities that otherwise appear in the astronomical model based on Newton's observations of earth's inner gravitational behaviour. But this presumed concession to Newton's belief in God is tendentious and deceptive on several counts. For one thing, it sets the conditions for the eventual and inevitable denial of this "God of the gaps," when subsequent astronomical and mathematical discoveries establish new kinds of regularities to put in the place of Newton's irregularities. In this spirit, certain theoretical physicists talk nowadays of the prospect of a "Theory of Everything." More seriously: the notion of the "Newtonian Universe" misrepresents Newton's faith in God, which was not something that he came to at the end of a mathematical calculation, but which stood on utterly different grounds.

It is the God of Abraham, Isaac and Jacob that Newton discusses in his theological compositions. He never tired of saying that the possibility of personal faith in God was open to all who conscientiously studied Scripture, even though, as already noted, he believed that only an elite had grasped Scriptures' deepest laws, and even though it was only the views of this learned elite that he cared to spend his own time on. For the established churches and their leaders, he had little patience. It was Newton's view, writes Frank Manuel, the foremost scholar of Newton's religion, that "To be constantly engaged in studying and probing into God's actions was true worship and fulfillment of the commandments of the Master ... Working in God's vineyard staved off evil, and work meant investigating real things in scripture, not fabricating metaphysical systems and abstractions ... Only two paths [for Newton, led to God:] the study of His actions in the physical world, His creations, and the study of the verbal record of His commandments in Scripture, both of which have an objective historical existence." [22]

Of the modern scholarly experts on Newton, Frank Manuel is virtually alone in insisting that Newton is entitled to respect for the investments of time that he made in this work. Louis Trenchard More gives much more notice than most to Newton's interests in theology in his biography of Newton, noting that "While the world will always regard his scientific work as an end in itself, he seems only to have felt it was a hard and dreary taskmaster, and not of intrinsic value, except as it should give evidence of the laws and attributes of God. It is altogether a mistake to suppose that his interest in religion served as a relaxation for his mind when exhausted by his scientific studies ... [He] read persistently in theology, and especially after he had forsaken science ... [He] wrote draught after draught of many of his papers for the sheer love of writing down his meditations ... However little value they may have in comparison with his scientific work they are not the fruit of a morbid state of mind. He did not turn to religion as a solace from discouragement or fear, but cultivated it steadily because he believed it to be the noblest occupation of the mind." Yet,

More does not disagree with the general verdict: that this activity is an embarrassment to the modern mind - "an utter waste of time," given that "Modern scholarship has proven conclusively the true character of Old Testament vision as vaticinium ex eventu ." [23]

Newton's scientific discoveries and what the "Newtonians" (following Voltaire) made of them helped to transform the religious outlook of the West. But Manuel conludes, this "would have mortified him". [24] Propagation of the "Newtonian" world-view encouraged the impression that one's grasp of God's role in the whole scheme of things gets clearer and more accurate the further we remove God from our awareness of self. And so eventually "Newton's God" ceased to be philosophically defensible. But it was not the God-of- the- gaps that Newton worshipped, and Whom he was seeking, in his way, to serve in all that herculean Biblical research. There are many ironies here. Had Newton been braver in putting forth his theological speculations in his own lifetime, it would not have been possible for his literary heirs to "hush up" the evidence (as Lord Maynard Keynes' puts it.) [25] Orthodox Christians would not have been pleased by the drift of Newton's whole eschatological scheme, especially his judgement on the history of the Church since what he called its "persecution" of Arius and its lapse into the "false teaching of the Trinity." But however much it might in the short run have distressed the Church to have the name of the greatest mind of the age attached to heretical views, it has done Christian faith vastly greater harm that the intellectuals, following Voltaire, have been able to suppress the evidence of Newton's commitment to a fundamentally supernaturalist, transcendentalist, theistic faith, grounded on what is nowadays called the "high view" of Scripture's historical and linguistic reliability - what outsiders call "Fundamentalism."

The issue here is not censorship of Newton's view: it was Newton himself who suppressed his own theological views in his own lifetime. What is at issue here is *the willful suppression, after his lifetime, by the whole world of learning, of the true nature of Newton's view of God, and of what we know and do not know on science's authority.* A totally false notion of Who was "Newton's God" took hold. It is not difficult to account for this virtually universal misconception. Newton's literary heirs and scientific epigoni, products of the new Enlightenment and governed by its contempt for all supernaturalism, were appalled to discover the evidence of all that literary labour in the vineyard of Prophecy; and, says Manuel, "for two hundred years thereafter most of the manuscripts were suppressed, bowdlerized, neglected, or sequestered, lest what we believed to be shady lucubrations tarnish the image of the perfect scientific genius." [26]

In very recent times, all of Newton's previously unpublished papers have been gathered together in the Yehuda Manuscript collection at the Hebrew University in Jerusalem, from the many scattered depositories into which they had sifted; and thus today serious scholars can take all the "shady lucubrations" into their accounts of Newton. There is no longer any excuse for the old red herring called "the Newtonian world-view" or "Newton's God of the gaps" to be dragged through the pages of the intellectual histories of his and the subsequent centuries. But a quick glance at any Western Civilization textbook will show you that it is.Unlike the case of Hal Lindsey and the popular eschatologists of our time, this is the case of the foremost mind of his century, almost universally conceded to have been such, then as now. But pornography is pornography, no less to be condemned when found in the possession of distinguished old gentlemen. In Newton's case, the evidence for his intellectual investments in Biblical eschatology is simply ignored, or dismissed, with a giggle, as the crochet of his senile years. What he himself had to say about his own priorities as a thinker is simply set aside as something like a nervous tick, which people of good breeding have the grace to overlook, for his sake! Never mind that Newton warned time and again of the perils of neglecting the study of Biblical prophecy: "Thou seest therefore that this is no idle speculation, no matter of indifferency, but a duty of the greatest moment." [27] And here he quoted the words of Jesus: "Ye Hypocrites! You know how to discern the face of the sky, but you cannot discern the signs of the times" (*Mt.* 16:2b.)

Chapter Five: Knowledge From the First Show.

> With regard to prophecy as foretelling,
> the church has lost its nerve.
> - Joyce Baldwin [28]

Jesus and the Prophets.

Again and again during His ministry, Jesus of Nazareth reminded His disciples that it was necessary for Him to fulfill all that the Prophets had said concerning Him. He must go to Jerusalem, He said, because there is in the history of Israel a precedent for the suffering and martyrdom of prophets in Jerusalem. [29] Jesus *times* His ascents to Jerusalem so that His appearances and actions there will *fit* into the patterns that associate the various festivals with various stages in the eventual realization of Israel's hopes for redemption. He *times* his last visit, and manages the details of his arrival (the foal, the palm branches, the entry through the prescribed gate) to match all the prophecies which are the pieces of the puzzle.

To an outsider, this sounds like a person whose actions are being wilfully directed so as to conform to a pattern. The inclination, therefore, is to say that the pattern is the *cause* and Jesus' deeds are the *response* to the pattern. This apparent requirement of logic prompts the vein of exegesis that sees

Jesus of Nazareth obsessed by a role that He is to play, given Him out of the past. He will act out all the features that recur in prophetic prophecies regarding David, the Son of David, the Servant, the Messiah. His acting-out of these prophetic elements will be the definitive acting-out; and God will honour this matchless gift of faith, and will intervene to rescue and to vindicate Him. Interpretations in this vein abound among the doubters and the cynics, but also are to be found among pious liberals of a mystical bent - Albert Schweitzer being the most striking example. [30]

Our options here are clear. If Jesus is *responding* to established historical patterns (the pattern of martyrdom of prophets in Jerusalem) and established patterns in prophetic foretelling (the expectation of Messiah's declaration of Himself in Jerusalem, the expectation of the people's welcoming of Him, the expectation, finally, of His rejection and suffering), then He requires no privileged access to the mind and purposes of God. If these details of his adventures, so to speak, can be read in advance out of the sacred texts, they could have been read, with equal success by someone else. The other option is that Jesus is what the Creed says He is. In this case, then His deeds are not to be thought of as the responses to the prophecies, but the prophecies have to be understood as responses to His deeds.

Seen in the context of this life-in-time, His deeds must of course be recognized as happening later than the prophecies of them. In time, things happen consecutively. It is not possible for later deeds to be causes of earlier deeds or thoughts. But in eternity, all human actions and their consequences are seen in their whole context. And all of God's responses to human actions are taken in the full knowledge of the full content of time. Thus, the covenant with Noah is already shaped by the covenant with Moses; the covenant with Abraham is already shaped by the covenant with Israel; and all of these are already shaped by the requirements of the life-history of Jesus of Nazareth. So is the history of Israel, its gathering, its scattering, its imperfect regathering *before* Jesus' time, its subsequent worldwide scattering *after* His life-time, its subsequent regathering in our own time, and its perfected gathering *in the Last Time*.

A Matter of Tenses.

In the days and hours prior to His crucifixion, Jesus spoke to his disciples of the end of all things and of the life to come. He spoke of all that would have to be "accomplished" within the Sacred History before the last things could begin. He spoke as though it had all been decided; as though it were already over - not just in principle, not just metaphorically or poetically, but in reality - as though somewhere it is already true that Satan and death have been defeated and the lion is already lying down with the lamb. He spoke as though it all followed necessarily from the known record, the inveterate behaviour of "the Jews": "If they do not hear Moses and the prophets, neither will they be convinced if some one should rise from the dead" (*Lk* 16:31, from the parable of the rich man and Lazarus). The Temple will be destroyed; indeed, it is already *"forsaken"* by God (*Lk* 13:35). Yet, in apparent contradiction to this, He seems at other times to speak as though in principle the future were still wide open. In Gethsemane, He expressed fear of the coming events ("... horror and dismay overcame him" [*Mk* 14:33 (*NEB*)]); and, as though the rest of the story were not already decided, He prayed: "Abba, Father ... all things are possible to thee; take this cup away from me." (14:36 [*NEB*]).

For the whole of the previous week He had preached unstintingly, His "tactics" ranging from tender appeal (*Lk* 13:34) to righteous anger (*Lk* 19:45-46, *Mt* 23:13). But why did He bother at all, if He could see the outcome already?

To the whole city He declares:

> "Therefore I send you prophets and wise men and scribes, some of
> whom you will kill and crucify, and some you will scourge in
> your synagogues and persecute from town to town, that upon you
> may come all the righteous blood shed on earth, from the blood of
> innocent Abel to the   blood of Zechariah the son   of Barachiah,
> whom you murdered between the   sanctuary and the altar. Truly, I
> say to you, all this will come upon this generation.
> "Jerusalem, Jerusalem, killing the prophets and stoning those
> who are   sent to you!   How often would I have   gathered   your
> children together as a hen gathers   her brood under her wings, and you
> would not!   Behold, your house is forsaken and desolate. For I tell
> you, you will not see me again, until you say, 'Blessed   is he who
> comes in the name of the Lord' " (*Mt* 23:34-39)

And then privately, to His disciples, He spoke of the Temple:

> "You see all these, do you not? Truly, I say to you, there will not
> be left here one stone upon another that will not be thrown down."
> As he sat on the Mount of Olives, the disciples came to him
> privately saying, "Tell us, when will this be, and what will be the
> sign of your coming and of the close of the age?"
> And Jesus answered them, "Take heed that no one leads you
> astray. For many will come in my name, saying, 'I am the
> Christ,' and they will lead many astray. And you will hear of wars and
> rumours of wars; see that you are not alarmed; for this must take
> place, but the end is not yet. For nation will rise against nation,
> and kingdom against kingdom,   and there will be famines and
> earthquakes in various places: all this is but the beginning of the
> sufferings.
> "Then they will deliver you up to tribulation and put you to
> death; and you will be hated by all nations for my name's sake.
> And then many will fall away, and betray one another, and hate one
> another. And many false prophets will arise and lead many astray.
> And because wickedness is multiplied, most men's love will grow
> cold. But he who endures to the end will be saved. And this gospel
> of the kingdom will be   preached throughout the whole world, as a
> testimony to all nations; and then the end will come.
> "So when you see the desolating sacrilege spoken of

by the prophet Daniel, standing in the holy place (let the reader understand), then let those who are in Judea flee to the mountains; let him who is on the housetop not go down to take what is in his house; and let him who is in the field not turn back to take his mantle.

"And alas for those who are with child and for those who give suck in those days! Pray that your flight may not be in winter or on a sabbath. For then there will be great tribulation, such as has not been from the beginning of the world until now, no and never will be. And if those days had not been shortened, no human being would be saved; but for the sake of the elect those days will be shortened.

"Then if any one says to you, 'Lo, here is the Christ!' or 'There he is!' do not believe it. For false prophets will arise and show great signs and wonders so as to lead astray, if possible, even the elect. Lo, I have told you beforehand. So, if they say to you, 'Lo, he is in the wilderness,' do not go out; if they say, 'Lo, he is in the inner rooms,' do not believe it. For as the lightning comes from the east and shines as far as the west so will be the coming of the Son of man. Wherever the body is, there the eagles will be gathered together.

"Immediately after the tribulation of those days the sun will be darkened, and the moon will not give its light, and the stars will fall from heaven, and the powers of the heavens will be shaken; then will appear the sign of the Son of man in heaven, and then all the tribes of the earth will mourn, and they will see the Son of man coming on the clouds of heaven with power and great glory; and he will send out his angels with a loud trumpet call, and they will gather his elect from the four winds, from one end of heaven to the other.

"From the fig tree learn its lesson: as soon as its branch becomes tender and puts forth its leaves, you know that summer is near. So also, when you see all these things, you know that he is near, at the very gates.

"Truly, I say to you, this generation will not pass away till all these things take place. Heaven and earth will pass away, but my words will not pass away. But of that day and hour no one knows, not even the angels of heaven, nor the Son, but the Father only ... Therefore you also must be ready; for the Son of Man is coming at an hour you do not expect" (Mt 24:2-36, 44.)

Here, in what is called the Synoptic Apocalypse (i.e., *Mt* 24 and parallels: *Mk* 13 and *Lk* 21), all the challenges that Jesus has to put to us, in our search for the elements of a faithful Philosophy of History, come into focus. If we have read the Gospels to this point with open hearts and minds, we are prepared for the sovereign liberty which Jesus takes here with regard to tenses. Speaking from the perspective of the God of Israel, He is able to say, "therefore I send you prophets (etc..)" in the present tense, while He reviews the whole course of Israel's dealings *in the past* with God's emissaries to Israel ("prophets, scribes, wise men, Zechariah ..." (23:34-5)); simultaneously, he speaks of Israel's *future* dealings with the disciples of the risen and ascended Jesus (" [when] you will kill and crucify ... [and] scourge in your synagogues and persecute from town to town" [23:34]). In that moment of time, a few days before the Crucifixion, He presents the account of the meaning of all human action, as He will present it at the moment of final judgement, after the End of History. "Truly," He says, this "will come" (shifting to the future tense, accommodating the perspective of His audience in this moment of time.) But, though future, it will come "upon this generation." Does "this generation" refer to the limited number who are standing around Him? Or does He speak of people of evil character, whenever they should hear these words of His, now and in the future - the whole sinful generation of mankind, who will answer to Jesus, before the throne of God (as seen in the *Book of Revelation* ,and *cf. John* 5:22-9)? Unless we allow for Jesus' access to the perspective of eternity, the perspective from which the whole content of time is seen and known, the words are senseless. Furthermore, it is morally indefensible to charge the present audience with the previous murders of Abel and of Zechariah the son of Berachiah, and the future murders of the saints of the Church - if we understand the present audience to be the limited number of live souls standing before Him that day, in that moment-of-time, in that place.

"How often would I have gathered your children ...," He laments, in the name of the God of Israel; for no one else but this God can be pictured in this way, reviewing the whole history of His own dealings with Jerusalem. But now, "your house is forsaken" (23:38) - assuming a point of present vantage on the events surrounding the destruction of the Temple, which *will occur* in 70 A.D., a generation after Israel's rejection of Him, and yet speaking to an audience even further away in time - the audience of all humanity, present before Him at the End of Time.Then, a staggering dislocation of perspective, looking to the Day of Israel's acceptance of Him, when "you" will say, "Blessed is he who comes in the name of the LORD" (23:39). This refers to "the Day of the LORD," spoken of by Old Testament prophets, the Day which Christians would subsequently look forward to as the Return of Christ, the Second Advent.

How do we deal responsibly with this matter of tenses? Given that this perspective - the perspective from which the whole content of time is known - is the privileged perspective of the Triune God; and given that Jesus is Himself so circumspect (*Mt* 24:36) about claiming it in the presence of His disciples before they have seen the Resurrection, and can begin to deal with its whole meaning - should we not conclude that these mysteries are not for us, and piously retreat? This might seem to be what Christian piety calls for, were it not that, quite apart from what Jesus is claiming here, and long before He was in the world claiming it, there were Prophets who also claimed to be speaking the Word of God from that perspective from which the whole content of time is known. The crucial difference between the Prophets and Jesus on this point is ineffably great: namely, that Jesus claims Himself to *come from* that Place. [31] He claims that his words have the authority of words of God, Who has knowledge of the full content of time. But the authority that Jesus claims does not diminish the authority of the Old Testament prophets. In fact, it enlarges it. Appealing to their words, He asks His hearers to see in the Prophets a capacity to speak of Him, and in their deeds to prefigure specific fulfillments of prophecies to be done by Him. [32] And in the light of this, His present listeners must see that here is one greater than Moses, greater than Elijah, [33] greater than all of them, because He is identical in authority with God Whose words the Prophets brought.

To understand the words of the Prophets, we have to grasp that what they spoke they spoke with the authority of the God of Israel Who sent them, in Whose "Name" they spoke judgement on this, blessing on that, words of knowledge about the future. Speaking under this burden, the Prophets find themselves shifting tenses without rational or grammatical justification.

Knowing the Whole Content of Time.

To grasp what follows in the next few paragraphs, there is a minimum age you have to be.

Sometime toward the end of THE WAR, when I was about ten, the Beaver Theatre in West Toronto one Saturday afternoon waived its admission price, as a contribution to the War Effort. For that day only (and never again since) the price of admission was a used pot or pan, contributed at the door to Canada's scrap metal drive. Not surprisingly, there was a huge line-up; and before we had worked up to the doors, the theatre was full. So we sent my kid sister home to ask Mother if we could stay for the Second Show.

For about an hour-and-a-half, we stood in line outside the door, which swung open at intervals, as the luckier kids of the First Show came out to buy treats or do the other. All this time we could hear the background music, sometimes more clearly than at other times. Occasionally, there were other more revealing clues, when the door briefly opened, and a line of dialogue was clearly heard. There might even be a quick glimpse of the action. Frequently, when the music became intense, louder, faster-moving, and trumpets figured in a big way, there were outbursts of gunfire. Once, the door opened at a point when the music was all strings, no brass; and there we caught a glimpse of Red Ryder prone on the ground, his head bloodied, and cradled by some obnoxious, interfering woman. His horse and Little Beaver could be glimpsed. Both were desolate. Towards the end of our long wait, the music was all crescendo, more and more brass. And then enough kids were coming out that the doors did not close fully again, and seats became available for the alert and the tough. And, thank God, there was Red Ryder and Little Beaver and the horse, all smiling, and the interfering lady nowhere in sight. The End.

Now we went in, and the Second Show would soon begin. Now we could begin to discover how this final blessed state of affairs came out of that evidently hopeless, violin-embedded earlier scene. Now we were going to see for ourselves what was the action that belonged to the moments of crescendo, and how the bad news of the long string passages gave way to the good news of the brass. Black hats that we had glimpsed once or twice when the doors parted, were now to be seen clearly. We would now see the exact villancies that they had done.

Or rather: that they were *going to do.*

Is it correct to say that Black Hat is *about to* shoot at Red Ryder, or that we now know that he *did* shoot at Red Ryder? Now it is spoiling our excitement a little that we also know that it is not fatal, as immediately appears. But that is only because we have the knowledge that we acquired in the lobby. Or rather, the partial knowledge - some glimpses from that place (the First Show) where the whole content of the film is already known. While we were out in line, we shared only meagre hints of the knowledge that belonged wholly to the First Show, insights given us as unexpected gifts from out of the treasury of the whole knowledge of the story which the First Show already has. Now inside, I do not envy them. That whole knowledge is already beginning to turn cold for them. But not for me. Still, it is a comfort (one which the First Show did not have) to know, before it began, how it all ends.

I have suggested that you have to be a certain minimum age to grasp the above - not because it is too hard, but because it is for younger generations too easy! It would be difficult to get across to those under our age that there are mysteries for logic and for imagination involved in what we went through, standing first outside and then inside. Young people today are entirely comfortable with the requirements of thought and imagination involved and will be unable to grasp the noetic challenge. Nurtured from their earliest recollection on movies, mostly seen at home, viewed through video-cassette recorder-players, they have learned at an early age the special conditioning of the imagination required by the narrative techniques of the film-makers. This has given them an inestimable advantage in dealing with what one might take the liberty of calling the "technical aspects" of prophecy.

For young people today, the challenges we all face in dealing with the claims of prophecy do not (or should not) turn on the problematics of tense. For example, the techniques of "flash-back" appeared early in film-making; but only recently has "flash-forward" become part of conventional "film narration." The movie-goer of my generation had to get used to this. The movie-watchers (that is, everybody) of the present generation got used to it in the cradle, and probably wonder what "getting used to it" could possibly mean. But the first time he encountered it as a child, the contemporary movie-watcher turned in puzzlement to someone older to find help with his confusion: We see these people, standing around at a party. But suddenly, they are standing at an open coffin, and inside is one of the characters, whom we have just now seen standing and talking and laughing. Now, everyone is again standing and talking and laughing in yet another setting, and there is the dead one, standing and talking and laughing with them, as before! The answer in childish terms is: That is something that is *going to happen* later. They are letting us see this now. Later, we will understand.

These techniques - flash-backward, flash-forward, slow-motion (preferred for moments of anguish, and for some reason with the sound-track turned off) are now routine features in the narrative technique of movies. Nobody above the age of six needs help with this anymore. But someone who had not seen a movie in twenty years would be completely at a loss with these routine devices.

*   *   *

Until recently, much that was "described" by the Prophets was, by all the canons of logic and natural philosophy, unvisualizable, and therefore seemed unreasonable. These things had to be (as they say) "taken on faith." Today (contrary to the usual line of argument) we are asked to "take on faith" much *less* than our ancestors. The inventions of modern technology have greatly eased for the modern person problems of imagination which were terribly forbidding to ancient people, and which remained so for everyone until recently. For example, radio and television and satellite communication and computer-enhancement and other blessings whose names I do not even care to know make it easy for us to visualize how "a sign" might, in the Last Day, appear to everyone everywhere in a moment-of-time (as, for example, Jesus seems to be requiring of us in *Mt* 24:27, 30, and as is required in key passages in several Old Testament prophecies and in *Revelation*). There is nothing at all "unreasonable" about this picture. No true problems of visualization or of logic attach to this picture *for us*; and anyone rejecting what is being said there on the ground of some alleged logical or scientific possibility is simply avoiding the real question about these claims: namely, the question of the authority by which Jesus claims to know these things. Are there allusions in Jesus' words here

(*Mt* 24:27, 30) to the specific "technology' with which we are familiar, and which makes it possible for us to envisage such events - allusions, that is, to television, satellites, etc.? I doubt this, although many Christians enthusiastically make these identifications, seeing in them vindications of the foreknowledge of Scripture. In any case, these possibilities are irrelevant to my present point: which is simply that we have no excuse for refusing to entertain the eschatological scenario on grounds of scientific or logical impossibility - grounds which for every generation previous to the First World War could be decently advanced. In our day, there have been occasions when up to one-third of the world's population has been watching and listening to *the same event in the same moment of time* - the grand opening of the Olympics, the funeral of Princess Diana. No *technical* obstacle prevented the *whole population* of the world from witnessing this event in the one moment-of-time, had some of us not chosen to be otherwise employed.

Even harder to grasp (even though small children are expected to handle this) is the fact that the number of images of such a single televised event is in any given dimension of space, however small, unlimited. One large television set sitting on a large table will give us one image and one voice. Twenty smaller T.V. sets on the same table would give us twenty identical images. No one knows the number of miniaturized receivers that might be fitted into this same space; but in theory (I am told by electronics experts) the number is finite! A single image is multiplied an unlimited number of times and this does not contradict the fact that it is one! How would anyone like the task of explaining this as a natural possibility to the contemporaries of John (the author of the Book of *Revelation*), or to Isaiah, or to Daniel, or Ezekiel?

Other examples of our theme are suggested by the videotape recorder. Again, toddlers all over our part of the cosmos have the handling of this technology mastered before they can read (if they ever can read). They know that the tape can be put in the VCR and the images started up at any point; that you can run it back and see the really good stuff again, or skip forward and avoid the boring stuff. Nor do they have the least difficulty grasping the limiting side of this: that the content of the action cannot be changed. You can manipulate the images indefinitely and rejoice in them or brood over them until Doomsday, but you will never change a bit (byte?) of the detail.

All of this gives us today a privileged insight into some of the mysteries that so deeply puzzled the deepest, brightest, most spiritual saints before our time. How can you reconcile scripture which speaks of God's foreknowledge, His fore-seeing of our actions, with the Bible's equally strong claim that our will is sovereignly free? Admitting that what the Bible says has to be taken on faith, these earlier saints conceded that it was impossible for us to visualize. For us today, it is not in the least impossible to visualize. Think of how many times one might re-run the VCR of the real film footage (which all of us have seen so often) of President Kennedy and his entourage heading down that Dallas road towards the Texas Book Depository. Who has not felt the anguish of wanting to intervene and get this stopped, to call out to President Kennedy or anybody else standing or sitting there, all of them smiling exuberantly (except the Secret Service men), to stop, go back, take another turn. You can flash that back, and you can skip it forward until you wear it out, but nowhere in all of its images is there one of a John F. Kennedy who steps out of the car.

Little children today grasp early (but not easily) the truth involved. *There are two time-dimensions.* To one of those we are spectators. Its whole content is known to us - that is, all the content of all the images. And the other is the one in which we are for this moment alive, and whose future content is radically open and undecided. There, on the screen, is an audience, moving along with Kennedy and the motorcade, spectators who appear along with the images of President Kennedy, and Mrs. Kennedy and Lyndon Johnson and Governor Connolly, and the others. The same familiar configured images are constantly changing; but always, unfailingly, and in every perfectly specific detail, changing in the same direction. New things (to them, but not to us) present themselves to that Dallas audience. In each moment, they are all radically ignorant of the configuration of images in the next moment. They cannot react as we react, anticipating the new things. Their lack of this foreknowledge is a fact in itself of the most radical significance. We can see the evidences of this ignorance in their faces: they are cheering, while we, knowing what comes now, are in dismay.

To say that we know how it ends, and that we know all the detail of all the actions taken by all the figures all along the way is in no way in contradiction of the other thing that we say: namely, that *they* , the participants, are in this moment of their participation radically free to act differently. In fact, having our perspective, we know their radical freedom to act much more clearly than they do (from our perspective, *did*) as they stand (*stood*) around thinking that they are (*were*) doing everything that needs (*needed*) doing. The dynamic behind these events is out of our control; but it is (*was*) not out of theirs. If we could imagine someone who had never heard of these events viewing this tape for the first time, we could also imagine surprise and horror. But *we* do not have these emotions anymore. We feel instead, futility, and a terrible mood of poignancy.

It is not in my view impious - rather, it is in a spirit of appreciation that God has made these insights available to our generation - to say that we have here with respect to these images and what they represent the *vantage* from which Jesus speaks in *Matthew* 23 and 24. We are dealing here with images, and not the content of those events. We are talking about resources for visualizing the content of Prophecy. We do not see the thoughts or the feelings or the emotions. Most of what was really there is as hidden to us in reviewing the films as it was to the participants. In eternity, all that is hidden will be disclosed (*I Corinthians* 4:5). But what we do see on the film we see from a privileged perspective: the perspective from which it is known *how it all ends*.

Frameworks of Prophecy.

As he sat on the Mount of Olives, the disciples came to him privately saying, "Tell us, when will this be, and what will be the sign of your coming and of the close of the age?" (*Mt* 24:3. Cf. *Mk* 13:3-4, *Lk* 21:7.)

Exegetes of equal scholarship, piety, and goodwill, sort out differently the time-framing of the predictions which Jesus then offers to the disciples. Most (but not all) agree that we are dealing with "frames" (in the plural), not a single "time-frame". A trustworthy current *Commentary on Luke*, that of Norval Geldenhuys, distributes the words of Jesus in this manner:

> So terrible, the Savior warns them, will be the judgements soon to burst forth over the people of Jerusalem who so persistently rejected Him that the events accompanying those judgements upon the guilty city will be the foreshadowing of the Final Judgement at His second advent. For this reason, Jesus' prophecies in connection with the events of the End- time are so closely linked up with those concerning the destruction of Jerusalem and the temple that it is extremely difficult in studying the Prophetic Discourse (*Matt.* xxiv and xxv; *Mark* xiii; *Luke* xxi. 5-36) to distinguish between the portions of it that refer to the Jews and Jerusalem and those referring to the Final Judgements at His second advent in power and glory ... [V]erses [*Lk*] 21:5-24 [parallel *Mt* 24:1-22] deal practically throughout (except verses 8, 9 [par. *Mt* 24:4-6]) with predictions concerning the destruction of Jerusalem and the preceding events, although in a secondary sense some of these predictions also refer to the Last Things. But in verses 25-8 [par. *Mt* 24:29-31] Jesus looks beyond the foreshadowings of the Final Judgements to that

Judgement itself and its attendant signs, in association with His second advent. In verses 29-33 [par. *Mt* 24:32-36] He exhorts His hearers to watch for the former set of events, which are to be accomplished within "this generation," while in verses 34-6 [par. *Mt* 24:42: "Watch therefore, for you do not know on what day your Lord is coming" He warns them (and through them the whole Christian church) to watch faithfully for the latter set of events, which are to take place at a day and hour known to none save God the Father. [34]

While accepting Geldenhuys' specific applications, we suggesst that we may also be permitted to see through more than one time-frame at once. Furthermore: just as the prospect enclosed in even the smallest frame widens as we draw it closer to our eye - so that when it touches the eye it will include the whole prospect before us - so a single one of the frameworks which appear in Jesus' prophecies can be made to enclose wider and wider prospects as we draw it closer - that is, as we hold it further away from the plane of life-in-time. What Jesus tells us here, He tells us from the perspective of One who knows the whole content of time: namely, the perspective of eternity. We can think of Him as holding in His hand an indefinite though still finite number of time-frames (since the content of time is finite), but holding them at an infinite distance from the plane of life-in-time. When we see this, we should also see at once that at an infinite distance any single time-frame, no matter how narrow, would serve to frame the whole of the content of time. So, we might as well assume that Christ holds in His hand, at an infinite distance, only one time-frame. It does not matter which time-frame it is, for at this infinite distance it serves as a framework for the whole content of life-in-time.

I have suggested that it helps us understand the perspective from which the Prophets know what they know of history if we think in terms of the possibilities of review and preview, flash-forward and flash-backward, which we all now grasp through the technology of movies and video-recording.

But that modest analogy breaks down after a little while. We need to add another dimension: we must also somehow imagine ourselves at an infinite distance from all the events of life-in-time - infinitely distant, and therefore *equally* infinitely-distant, from all the events of life-in-time, recorded on one all-inclusive videotape. We should try to imagine that we hold in our hand a single frame, which we have originally designed so that, when held up to the surface of ordinary life-in-time it enclosed, for example, the years 1939 to 1945 A.D. But now, we hold this at an infinite distance from that single video-taped record of the whole content of life-in-time, and looking through it, we see that it now frames the whole of life-in-time!

(What I have said here also may also make sense as *physics*. But let us not get over our heads!) [35]

When Jesus speaks in the present or even the past tense of events which to His hearers were *not yet*, he is not indulging in a manner-of-speaking. Nor is He "taking liberties." We see this same sort of *apparent* taking-of-liberties frequently in Old Testament prophecy. The knowledge which the Prophet claims to have is of some future content of this life-in-time, but seen from the perspective from which it is known how *all* event-in-time concludes. It is something glimpsed from the First Show. If one does not grasp that knowledge of this kind is in the Bible, then one falls into the mistake of saying that these people are taking liberties, or that these are rhetorical devices or literary figures.

When, for example, Isaiah (in *Isaiah* 7:1 to 8:10) prophesies so urgently to the Kings and the people of Israel about the coming Assyrian menace, he has in view a specific period of time, roughly eighteen months to two years. He has been shown that within this span of time the leaders must turn around, seek the will of God, and begin to make wise decisions. Likewise the people, within this same frame of time, must also seek the will of God, put behind their selfishness and gluttony, and discover the needs of the poor in their midst. To illustrate the urgency of this, and to underline that a specific crisis is in view - that Isaiah is not just sermonizing about recurring and generalized truths - the prophet speaks of a child who is born somewhere in the Kingdom at that moment (7:14-16). Before that child grows old enough to tell the difference between right and wrong, the crisis will have occurred: it will then be too late to repent. Then, the prophecy is doubled: in 8:1-4, we are told that the message is acted out, illustrated, presumably, by Isaiah himself, who, on instruction from the LORD, "went to the prophetess, and she conceived and bore a son" (8:3), to whom the LORD has already assigned a name: "Call his name Maher-shalal-hashbaz [the spoil speeds, the prey hastens], for before the child knows how to cry 'My father' or 'My mother,' the wealth of Damascus and the spoil of Samaria [the Northern Kingdom, Israel] will be carried away before the king of Assyria." But already Isaiah has been given to see, from that perspective where the *whole content of time* is known, that Israel will not turn back to God. He sees already the conquest of Israel, by Assyria, which will be accomplished by stages, and the captivity and transportation of the population, beginning with the northernmost tribes, Zebulun and Naphtali (Galilee.) Now his inspiration is taken up several octaves, and he is able to say something that, while it seems to be a description of those events, cannot *merely* be that, because it talks about a glorious outcome to all of this, an outcome which does not belong within the presumed framework - the framework that encloses the span of time for a child to be conceived, born, and raised to the point where he knows right from wrong, and can call for his Mother and Father:

> But there will be no gloom for her that was in anguish. In the former time he brought into contempt the land of Zebulun and the land of Naphtali, but in the latter time he will make glorious the way

of the sea, the land beyond the Jordan, Galilee of the nations.

The people who walked in darkness have seen a great light; those who dwelt in a land of deep darkness, on them has light shined. Thou hast multiplied the nation, thou hast increased its joy ....

For to us a child is born,to us a son is given;and the government will be upon his shoulder,and his name will be called,

"Wonderful, Counselor, Mighty God,

"Everlasting Father, Prince of Peace."

Of the increase of his government and of peace there will be no end, upon the throne of David, and over his kingdom,to establish it, and to uphold it with justice and with righteousness from this time forth and for evermore. The zeal of the LORD of hosts will do this (*Isaiah* 9:1-3a, 6-7.)

It is as though the frame which encloses this picture of the new human life conceived, born, and raised to the age of a young child, is now being held out at some enormous distance from the plane of life-in-time, so that centuries can be seen through it. And in the span of these centuries we see the tribes of Zebulun and Naphtali and then all of Israel carried off into captivity - but then brought back, and the life of the nation resumed, and a King once again set over them. But this is not a King like any before, and the society He presides over is not like any society they have ever known, or indeed like any that has been seen on earth. It is the Messianic Kingdom.

We have to understand that Isaiah sees all of this not by setting aside the frame of the original prophecy, but by holding that very same framework further and further away from the plane of life-in-time, so that through it he sees longer and longer vistas of future history, until he sees the Messianic Kingdom at the end of time. The *framework itself* still circumscribes the span of conception of a singular human life, and the birth and the nurturing of a human child until that child has reached the age of ability to speak and to learn. Such a framework, containing the story of an infant life, contains also the story of the Redemption of Israel. This is true now in eternity. Even now, in eternity, it is seen that this Child has the name (reputation) *"Immanuel," "God with Us"* (7:14), *"Wonderful, Counselor, Mighty God, Everlasting Father, Prince of Peace."*

Again, the crucial parts of the Prophecies of Isaiah with respect to the fall of Jerusalem, the evacuation of the royal and noble families of Judah, and the destruction of Solomon's Temple (*Isaiah*, Chaps 39 to 48) - events which lie a century and more later than his prophetic words - fit within a specific number of months (which our contemporary scholars can locate with quite remarkable accuracy, by the standard of Ancient History generally.) Everything that is said there is viewed through a timeframe that begins with the Babylonian capture of the Royal Family (c. 605 B.C.), follows through the later insurrection under Zedekiah (587), the subsequent destruction of the walls and the Temple, the beginning of the Babylonian captivity (586), the span of the captivity, the raising up of Cyrus (c. 539), and the return of the Jews to Jerusalem (following 538.) But the more one pours over these passages the more it becomes obvious that what is being said applies not merely to the events of those years. Things are being said, in higher octaves, or perhaps in the sequence of overtones above the pitch at which the narrative of those few months is sounded, about longer spans of time. We are told about the return from the captivity in Babylon, an event which is itself still more than a century away when Isaiah offers this prophecy, but lies within the immediate application of the timeframe. But we are also told about the *Return* to the land of Israel of generations of Jews yet to come, who are seen to be in captivity in places all around the globe to which no Jews have yet gone in the days of Isaiah (e.g., *Is.* 49, and *cf. Ezekiel* 36:16ff, *Deuteronomy* 28:62ff.) None of this can be found within the framework, when it is held up directly to the plane of life-in-time.

When a specific passage of prophecy provides a framework which clearly circumscribes the events belonging to a literal and specific and limited range of time, it is necessary for us to visualize it as having that "length": that is, two years, seven years, forty years, seventy years, four hundred years. Holding the time-frame in question directly up to the plane of life-in-time, we find that it both circumscribes and to some degree describes the content of a specific span of history. In this spirit, Daniel (*Daniel* 9) took the framework of Jeremiah's prophecy, uttered prior to the Babylonian invasion of Judah (esp., *Jeremiah* 25:11ff, and 29:1-14), and held it up to his own time (nearly seventy years later), and began to prepare for the political and religious opportunities that would follow upon the overthrow of Babylon - which event did indeed come suddenly, and within the framework of Jeremiah's prophecy, and which was (as Isaiah had foretold) the work of "Cyrus" (*Isaiah* 44 and 45.)

Abraham was given a quite specific and realistic prophecy regarding the whole process of history (*Gen* 12:1-3), which was subsequently restated (*Gen* 17:1-8; 22:16-18). But this prophecy has little empirical content in it. It serves as an overview of the course of history. If held up at any distance from the plan of history, it yields generalizations about the shape and character of the History of Israel, and recurring themes within it. And if held at an infinite distance, it yields the largest theme of history, the "universal way" of which Augustine wrote. Then later, in *Genesis* 15:13-14, we read: "The LORD said to Abram, 'Know this for certain, that your descendants will be aliens living in a land that is not theirs; they will be slaves, and will be held in oppression there for four hundred years. But I will punish that nation whose slaves they are, and after that they shall come out with great possession' " [NEB.] This prophecy stands between the foundation-prophecy of *Gen*. 12:1-3 and the first of many re-affirmations (including, *Gen*. 17:1-8). It adds unexpected features to the foundation-prophecy, without abridging any part of it. There is an easily-applicable time-framework, and the explicit instruction to hold it up to a four hundred years span of time, which the descendants of Abraham will recognize when they see it. It was in the light of this prophecy that Moses and subsequent generations understood their national experiences (*cf. Exodus* 12:40-41, and *I Kings* 6:1.) [36]

Moses, in the course of his final address to the people of Israel (*Deuteronomy*, Chaps 27-31), as they were preparing to enter Canaan without him, is brooding on this captivity-experience which they should have been putting behind them. They have behaved in the wilderness as though "captivity" had become ingrained in their spirits. He fears that there is more captivity to come, unless they can shake off the habits of fear, the inclination to subject themselves to gods of darkness which became so evident in the wilderness years. Is it possible that the experience of the years in Egypt, an experience of a fixed and specific length of time, foretold by God to Abraham, which was once part of their future and is now their recent past, has nonetheless some *remaining* application? Is the prophecy of the four hundred years perhaps a framework (like Isaiah's later prophetic framework of the Child called Immanuel), that is to be held up at a distance from the plane of real life-in-time, so as to yield *typical* meanings, *patterns* of recurring experience that lie ahead? But it would be too distressing for Moses and for the people to accept the logical drift of this evidence. Let the future remain radically open then, says Moses, and let us hold up the framework of the four hundred years of captivity merely as a cautionary model. Remember this experience of captivity and remember that it had been foretold to Abraham by the LORD, and has therefore the character and the authority of something known from the perspective of eternity. This recollection will encourage obedience to the commandments of God, and ward off the otherwise inevitable outcome: "If you will obey the LORD your God by diligently observing all his commandments which I [Moses] lay upon you this day, then the LORD your

God will raise you high above all nations of the earth, and all these blessings shall come to you and light upon you, because you obey the LORD your God." The specific character of all the blessings that contribute to private and social peace are then spelled out (28:1-14 [NEB]). "But if you do not obey the LORD your God by diligently observing all his commandments and statutes which I lay upon you this day, then all these maledictions shall come upon you and light upon you." And the specific maledictions follow (28:15-68), culminating in this:

> Then you who were countless as the stars in the sky will be left few in number, because you did not obey the LORD your God. Just as the LORD took delight in you, prospering and increasing you, so now it will be his delight to destroy and exterminate you, and you will be uprooted from the land which you are entering to occupy. The LORD will scatter you among all peoples from one end of the earth to the other, and there you will worship other gods whom neither you have known nor your forefathers, gods of wood and stone. Among those nations you will find no peace, no rest for the sole of your foot. Then the LORD will give you an unquiet mind, dim eyes, and failing appetite. Your life will hang continually in suspense, fear will beset you night and day, and you will find no security all your life long. Every morning you will say, "Would God it were evening!, and every evening, "Would God it were morning!", for the fear that lives in your heart and the sights that you see. The LORD will bring you sorrowing back to Egypt by that very road of which I said to you, "You shall not see that road again" (28:62-68a).

Then, in effect, the address is repeated (*Dt.* Chaps 29 and 30), beginning with the reminder of God's pledge to Abraham and the fact of God's written covenant with the people of Israel at Sinai. But this time, Moses moves virtually at once to the consequences of disobedience to the covenant (beginning 29:18). Particularly galling to his listeners that day must have been the passage (29:22-28) in which he speaks of the other nations, many generations later, contemplating the low estate to which the people of Israel will by then have been brought: all the nations will ask: " 'Why has the LORD so afflicted this land ...?' The answer will be: 'Because they forsook the covenant ... The anger of the LORD was roused again that land ... The LORD uprooted them from their soil in anger, in wrath and great fury, and banished them to another land, where they are to this day' " (29:24-28.) Then,

> When these things have befallen you, the blessing and the curse of which I have offered you the choice, if you and your sons take them to heart there in all the countries to which the LORD your God has banished you, if you turn back to him and obey him heart and soul in all that I command you this day, then the LORD your God will show you compassion and restore your fortunes. He will gather you again from all the countries to which he has scattered you. Even though he were to banish you to the four corners of the world, the LORD your God will gather you from there, from there he will fetch you home. The LORD your God will bring you into the land which your forefathers occupied, and you will occupy it again; then, he will bring you prosperity and make you more numerous than your forefathers were. The LORD will circumcise your hearts and the hearts of your descendants, so that you will love him with all your heart and soul and you will live (30:1-6 [NEB]).

Later (*Dt* 31:14-21), the LORD speaks privately to Moses and Joshua together, out of the hearing of the people: "Now write down this rule of life and teach it to the Israelites; make them repeat it, so that it may be on record against them ... For even before I bring them into the land which I swore to give them, I know which way their thoughts incline already" (*Dt* 31:19, 21a [NEB])." Without preamble, Moses has stepped across several thresholds. Beginning from a point of view that required him to admit ignorance of the future ("*if, ... but if no*"), he is now impelled by his brooding on the chapter of captivity in Egypt and the sad record of the people's unfaithfulness in the wilderness, to incline towards the worst-case scenario: It seems to be required as a matter of reasoning: *I know which way their thoughts incline already.* In this spirit, he speaks thoughtfully and grimly of the likely outcome in the immediately following generations. But as he speaks, he is caught up in an experience of prophetic   foreknowledge, and he finds himself plunging ahead to describe features of the story of generations well beyond those. He describes the scattering that follows the story of the settling of Canaan, which has not yet begun!   Between that remote future time and this present lies the conquest of Canaan, the regime of Joshua, the age of the Judges, Samuel, Saul, David, Solomon, the divided monarchy, the Assyrian conquest, and the Babylonian conquest. And most astonishing of all, there is a vision of scattering to *the four corners of the world.*" And then he steps through an even further threshold, and from there he sees that *"from the four corners of the world ... the LORD your God will gather you from there, from there he will fetch you home .."* (30:3-3.) He is no longer speaking of the open-ended future, but of the whole Plan of World History.

Moses began his address looking, as *we* normally do, into the open-ended future, offering predictions based upon reason and observation of the past, generalizing and extrapolating from the record of people's behaviour. But eventually it dawns on us as we read that he is taking liberties with tenses. He is speaking in the past tense of what can only be seen from that perspective where the content of the future is known. It is knowledge from the First Show. It is no longer *"if"*, but *"when these things have befallen you."* (30:1); and he is not really addressing present company anymore, but a generation which is already in renewed captivity (*"in all the countries to which the LORD your God has banished you ..."* [30:1]); and he is now putting before this yet unborn generation the open-ended options: *"If ... but if not ...,"* just as he is even now putting them before his own contemporaries on the day of his prophetic address, before their entry into Canaan!

At this most exalted pitch of prophetic foreknowledge, where everything is overtones, all out of reach of normal hearing, Moses is speaking in absolute concert with the Prophets of the exile: that is, the immediate forerunners and then the contemporaries of the still-unborn generations of the Babylonian Captivity. And he is speaking in absolute concert as well with Jesus of Nazareth, as He speaks to His disciples that day on the Mount of Olives. In these words of Moses, as in Jesus' words that day, the theme we hear in the overtones is the theme of ultimate Return - the definitive Return, that puts finish to all the chapters of captivity and scattering that are seen when Moses holds up in the middle distance the framework of the four hundred years which God originally gave to Abraham. But the people of the age of definitive Return are not like the people Moses knew in the wilderness. They are people restored to perfect obedience to the will of God. This Restoration is not their doing, however: they are people whose hearts God Himself has circumcised, [37] "so that you will love him with all your heart and soul and you will live" (30:6.)

*   *   *

When we approach prophecy, we must bring a spirit of submission to what is taught within the Scriptures of the Old and the New Testaments, and to what has been taught throughout the history of the Church. All prophecy has some *primary* application: i.e., it provides a framework circumscribing and to varying degrees describing some part of the content of a specific portion of future time. The dimensions of the various time-frames, and thus the dimensions of the content circumscribed vary tremendously. Some timeframes are very narrow: like *Isaiah* 7 and 8, the Child/Immanuel framework, which speaks of only a few months, perhaps three or four years. Sometimes, we find in the primary application a number or a figure which has *symbolical* value as well: *seven* is a week, and *seven sevens* (i.e., seven times seven, a week of weeks), or *forty* (which typifies exile or a time apart), or *seventy*. But quite apart from all the symbolical and typical possibilities, the numbers have primary and literal applications in some specific portion of historical time. *Daniel* abounds in these.

In addition to its primary application, a prophetic framework may have *secondary* applications. The original prophet often gives us the clues to such secondary applications of his prophecy. Thus, some prophetic frameworks are held out by their original prophets at one or more intermediate distances between the plane of life-in-time and eternity, so that they yield generalized or recurring truths about the course of history. And sometimes we see the original prophet holding his prophetic framework in imagination at an infinite distance from the plane of life-in-time, so that through it the *whole content of time* is seen. The framework then has the character of circumscribing or defining an ultimate or definitive theme - a theme that will be yielded up in the Last Day, at history's end, when we have the whole record of history, when the whole content is completed. Thus, Isaiah held out the framework of the prophecy regarding the Child/Immanuel to infinity and through it saw truths about the whole Plan of Redemption, the truths which Christians see realized in the Conception and the Birth and the Life of Jesus of Nazareth.

But is it clear that *all* prophetic frameworks are to be used by us in these ways - i.e.: (a) to be held at intermediate distances, so as to yield recurring truths about World History; and (b) to be held imaginatively at the distance of infinity, to yield definitive truth about how it will look in the End? One thing *is* clear: we should never think we are at liberty to hold up a particular framework anywhere and everywhere at will in the middle distance or at the imagined distance of infinity, unless we have first settled what is its *primary* application in the plane of life-in-time. If one refuses on principle the possibility of supernaturally-given specific foreknowledge of the content of history, one should not mess with prophecy at all. We have no right to think up other *applied* uses of prophecy, when we deny the thing that the prophet is most conspicuously claiming about himself, his message, and its Source: namely, that the knowledge he has is from the First Show, where the whole content of World History is known. By "primary application," I have in mind what Daniel has in mind in *Daniel* 9, where he is seen pouring over what we can also read in *Jeremiah* 25 and 29; and what Jesus is described as doing in *Matthew* 24, where He pours over what He has read and what we can also read in *Daniel* 11 and 12. The unbending practice in academic scholarship for the past century and more has been to deny the primary applications of prophecy. In this company, one never permits a prophetic framework to touch the surface of history - which amounts to refusing to concede that there is such a thing as supernaturally-given foreknowledge of specific events to come, which the original and the subsequent hearers were meant to watch for and to act upon (as Daniel is pictured as watching for and acting upon the specifics of Jeremiah's prophecy; and as Jesus tells his disciples and us to look for and act upon the specifics of Daniel's prophecy about "the abomination of desolation.") Academic scholarship prefers to dismiss instances of apparent foreknowledge as tricks done with mirrors: the text comes after the event, and is attributed to a distinguished figure who actually lived long before the event. This is called *vaticinium ex eventu* - in effect, *pretending* to "predict" what is in reality all finished and spread out before you in the record of history. In plain terms, pious fraud.

Yet perversely, these same scholars will make edifying use of the alleged prophecies by holding them up at a middle distance from the plane of time, so that through them one takes the liberty of seeing recurring themes, generalized truths, typical features of World History, or sometimes occasions for "prophetic" sermons on moral themes. The same author who tells you that there is fraud in the attribution of the text and that the alleged prophecy is in effect phony, now tells you that this deeply sensitive religious spirit has profoundly important things to teach us about (usually) our attitudes to the poor and the oppressed. Some theologians have virtually displaced the original content of the word "prophet," so that it has come to mean a speaker for social concerns. A "prophetic" message is thus one about current social and economic problems!

There is a simple test that applies here, and it is a moral one. If we cannot accept that there are possibilities of foreknowledge of the kind that certain characters in Scripture claim to have, from Abraham forward, then we have to subtract something very considerable from Scripture's authority to speak to us. If we say that there does not now exist and never has existed knowledge of the sort that the Old Testament Prophets claim to have (or that the hypothetical "editors" of their words attribute to them), then we say that *we* have a point of philosophical and moral advantage from which we study and judge what they say. We foreclose *ab initio* the possibility that we shall be contradicted, that we shall be told with authority something that we otherwise could not know. This assumption permits us to distance ourselves from the authors of the Biblical text so as to be "comfortable" with it. We merely say, in this situation, that we know from better authority, scientific and philosophical authority, that such things do not happen. It is from this point of vantage, logically and morally, that we then say that we are equipped to judge what can be rescued or redeemed from this scientifically and philosophically flawed text. In doing this, obviously, we are using criteria that are not intrinsic to the text but extrinsic to it - criteria regarding what it is possible to know and what is worth knowing, and notions of how we recognize these worthwhile things when we see them. These criteria and these notions we have brought to the text. The circularity of this reasoning is what saves us from being told anything authoritative by the text itself. This approach simply puzzles the conservative scholar, because it seems so pointless. It seems to eliminate the reason for reading Scripture. It forecloses in advance the possibility of being taught by Scripture or chastened by it.

These scholars do not hesitate to claim that the voice speaking to us is not the voice whose authority is clearly attached, by the text itself, to its message. It is not Moses, we are told, who is the source of this long-range prophecy (*Deuteronomy* , Chaps 27 to 31), with its perspective of range upon range of generations to come, and its moments of insight into the Messianic kingdom. Rather, it is the voice of a "Priestly Editor," centuries later than Moses, who sees what will calm the hearts and minds of his contemporaries, and puts such words into the mouth of the long-gone Moses, so as to convey a magic quality, a quality of supernatural authority, to truths that, needless to say, Moses could not have seen, any more than we can see the events of the Twenty-Fifth Century A.D. We are told that along the way from the first uttering of whatever (if anything) Moses, Joshua, Samuel, Amos, Micah, Isaiah, Jeremiah, Ezekiel, Daniel, Obadiah, Zechariah, *et. al.*, uttered, well-intending souls of deep learning and deepest piety (and usually of extraordinary "poetic" gifts, requisite for giving their "prophetic utterances" the literary thrust they would need to carry through subsequent edition and re-edition), *invented* magical and edifying things for them to say. We are given two, three, and by some authorities more voices behind the figure of Isaiah - originally a late Eighth Century B.C. figure who is presumed not to have known any more of the content of the history of the times of which he appears to prophesy (down to the late Sixth Century, letting alone the fulfillments which Christians claim to see in the life and death and resurrection of Christ!) than George Washington could have foreknown of the Presidency of Bill Clinton. Again, we are told of sovereignly self-confident

Second Century B.C. writers, with extraordinarily brilliant gifts of poetic imagination, who *reworked* the materials of the political life of their own time as pretended "prophecies" of a certain Daniel (probably fictitious in any case), supposed to have been in the court of Babylon with the first exiles, in the first half of the Sixth Century. And so on. [38]

Not all of us are equipped to deal with the technical questions of language, textual criticism, and so on that are invoked in these discussions. But we should not, without at least some resistance, go along quietly, as the majority of theological undergraduates politickly do, when we are told that there is a settled *scholarly consensus* in these matters. What there is, in fact, is a settled *policy* of denigration of scholarship which proceeds from a point of confidence in supernatural possibilities, but which is equally competent, when not more competent, in the technical disciplines involved. Where this all gets downright offensive is when we are told that this long history of pious gerrymandering of the properties and reputations of Old Testament saints has resulted in texts that are Great Religious Monuments - "Great" by some measurement that Abraham, Moses, Joshua, Isaiah, and the others, needless to say, never thought of. We must be infinitely patient with the text of *Daniel*, we are told, because of its Greatness of Vision or of Soul or of Literary Genius. Think how great must have been the soul of the anonymous man or men behind the voice of "Daniel," who has this truly monumental gift for cheering people up, and who hit upon the heart-warming device of attaching his (their) otherwise unpublishable visionary poetry to the reputation of Daniel (or Moses or Isaiah)! This is the point where this exercise of sovereign distancing from the authority of the text gets beyond being merely superfluous (and therefore boring) and becomes offensive. These scholars set their moral standards much too low, for our taste. We cannot bring ourselves to feel the gratitude they feel for these "gifts" of poetic imagination. Why should we? They are, after all, all around us. There is a long and rich (and well worthwhile) legacy of literary invention which belongs entirely to us and is in our own language, and for which we do not have to freeload upon long-dead ancient people. If this is what passed for literary and historical integrity in Ancient times, we do not wish to stoop so low (morally speaking). Certainly we should prefer to go else where for instruction in Philosophy of History, our present concern.

It is not in defense of "fundamentalism" (a word whose content I used to think I knew) or of "literalism" (*ditto*) that I argue here that one should not trust for any large purpose texts that wilfully deceive us about their provenance. We can grasp that there are such things as literary conventions, including the convention of pseudonymous authorship. But we assume that precisely because they were conventional, they could not deceive! Every age has some such conventions. We permit governments to churn out thousands of pages of text everyday, nominally the product of the mind of President Bill Clinton or Queen Elizabeth II, "signed" by these persons as though they were the true literary creators. But of the staggering pile of documents that appeared this week above the "signature" of Bill Clinton, we can assume that the same Bill Clinton has actually read, let alone created, very little. There is no intent to deceive here; there is, instead, a certain necessary legal fiction. On the day of their Fiftieth Wedding Anniversary, my parents received a telegram from the Governor-General of Canada, who said that they were very much on his heart that day. They were not "deceived" by this; nor was Governor General Edward Schreyer intending to deceive them. They were, in fact, and quite properly, pleased. We know that there are lines between conventional liberties and the intent to deceive. The matter is by no means as sophisticated as the scholars make it out to be. We have no difficulty grasping that Solomon could not have been the author of all the wisdom literature to which his name is assigned. And we agree that the Enoch of Genesis did not write the *Apocalypse of Enoch*; we doubt that there ever was a grown person in the world who believed that he did.

.People in ancient times dealt with the conventions involved as my parents dealt with the question of the Governor-General's telegram, or as the First World War draftee dealt with the question of the authorship of the letter bearing "Greetings" from Woodrow Wilson. But we think we know when we are being had, and we have no reason to think that the Ancient Jews were less bright than we are. To accept what the liberal scholars claim to be the *explanations* behind the authorship attributed to Isaiah and to Daniel, you have to agree to make honourable and edifying material out of patchworked fraud. Any grown person would prefer to get his guidance for life, let alone the materials for his Philosophy of History, from less morally-flawed sources.

Liberal scholars who claim to have taken up a higher moral and intellectual vantage-point with respect to Prophetic literature, have in fact lowered both the moral and the intellectual tone of theology. They have not found out a higher truth: they have, as Joyce Baldwin rightly says, merely lost their nerve.

Jesus' Teaching on *Daniel.*

When we are dealing with the words of Jesus, the stakes are, for Christians, vastly higher. Consider what creedal Christianity says of the authority of Jesus Christ. Either these passages have authority to shape our whole vision of world history, or they are mischievous fraud. There is no middle ground here.

It is no answer to those who believe in the predictive force of Prophecy to say that it is dangerous. Everything that works is dangerous. When "Krazy Glue" came onto the market about thirty years ago, people showed up in job lots at Emergency Departments of hospitals with terrible injuries caused by ignoring the label's clear warnings - that it really does seal just about immediately just about anything to just about anything else, including one's own skin. What was going on of course was that since the dawn of time we had all been discounting the lucid and explicit but false claims of the manufacturers of glue. We had lost our trust in the possibility that a statement on the label of a jar of glue might be true. If you applied it correctly, it was useless; but at least if you applied it incorrectly it was harmless. So, when Krazy Glue appeared a hue and cry went up that it was too dangerous for us, and should be put out of our reach. But mercifully, good sense prevailed and we have all had to learn to use the product with the respect that should attach to anything that works as it says it does.

In this same spirit we reject the lock-step advice of the academic theologians on this matter of eschatology. If it is true that speculation on End Times has done great damage in the past and is stirring up much trouble in the present, this is because it is about something real. It is dangerous because it works. It works because it is real. Of Jesus' call to us to watch for "the signs of the times," Isaac Newton rightly said: "This is no idle speculation, no matter of indifferency, but a duty of the great moment."

*   *   *

Jesus had announced the coming destruction of the Temple, and then had left the appalled audience, in the company of His disciples. Apparently He had already a fixed practice of gathering His disciples on the Mount of Olives for teaching on those aspects of His message that were not yet to be shared with the people. As with everything else that was happening in that week, there is a prophetic significance in the choice of site. The prophet Zechariah, speaking of the events of the End of Time, had promised that "on that day his feet will stand on the Mount of Olives ..." (*Zechariah* 14:4.) Thus, even before a word is uttered, we are disposed to see that the message is about the remainder of Israel's history and the End of Times. To make the point clearer, Jesus, in *Mt.* 24:15ff, deliberately draws the disciples' recollection to specific language from the prophecy of Daniel. Jesus' use of the phrase, "the abomination of desolation," explicitly evokes *Daniel* in three places (*Dn* 9:27, 11:31, 12:11.) He takes for granted that they believe that the passages in question derive from the historical figure of that name, Daniel, and that they have the force of supernaturally-inspired foreknowledge of the outcome of Israel's history. In His own use of this prophecy, He confirms the Jewish people's confident investments in it, and at the same time asserts His own claim to *authority which surpasses that of Daniel and all the prophets* ! Questions involved in these texts are about to be answered. Mysteries are about to be resolved.

In one of the passages from *Daniel* evoked by Jesus' words in *Matthew* 24:15, Daniel speaks of the last "week" (literally, seven) of seventy weeks (seventy sevens). The first sixty-nine sevens will have seen the regathering of the scattered people of Israel and the rebuilding of Jerusalem. The beginning of the last (the seventieth) of the sevens, is marked by the appearance of "one who is anointed." but who is "removed with no one to take his part; and the horde of an invading prince shall work havoc on city and sanctuary" (*Dan* 9:26-7 [NEB].) Then, "The end of it shall be a deluge, inevitable war with all its horrors. He shall make a firm league with the mighty [or, "with many"] for one week; and, the week half spent, he shall put a stop to sacrifice and offering. And in the train of these abominations shall come an author of desolation; then, in the end, what has been decreed concerning the desolation will be poured out.(*Daniel* 9:26a-27 [NEB].) Then, in a later vision (Chaps 10 to 12) Daniel is given a prophecy of extraordinary detail - of such extraordinary and colourful detail, indeed, that liberal scholarship rejects categorically the possibility that it comes from the mouth a Sixth Century B.C. figure; indeed, that it could be anything other than *vaticinium ex eventu*: "prophecy" after (or "out of") the event. The events in question clearly, almost transparently, belong to the period beginning with the overthrow of the Persian Empire by Alexander [333 B.C.] (11:2-3), following through the dynastic struggles and division of his empire on his death [323-280 B.C.] (11:4-5), then coming to focus in great detail (11:6-39) on the history of the conflict between the two successor Empires (that of the Seleucids, based in Syria, and that of the Ptolemies, based in Egypt). [39] In the contest between these two, the Land of Israel was one of the great prizes. As this dynastic struggle comes to its climax, we see the Jewish religious leadership intriguing to make the best of the opportunities afforded by shifts in the political situation (*Dan* 11:14f). There will be reckless popular leaders (11:14), and there will be scheming priests (11:20-22). In the last hours before losing Judah, the King of the North (usually identified with Antiochus IV ("Epiphanes") [176-163 B.C.]) will work out his rage against the Jews: "At the appointed time he will once more overrun the south, but he will not succeed as he did before. Ships from the West " [Heb.: "Ships of Kittim" (cf., *Numbers* 24:23-24.)] [40] will sail against him, and he will receive a rebuff. He will turn and vent his fury against the Holy Covenant; on his way back he will take due note of those who have forsaken it. Armed forces dispatched by him will desecrate the sanctuary and the citadel and do away with the regular offering. And there they will set up 'the abominable thing that causes desolation' " (*Dn* 11:29-31 [NEB].)

I have argued already that we have no right to make *applied* uses of prophecy, no matter how edifying or uplifting, unless we first deal with the *primary*. Jesus' contemporaries saw these prophecies (and the apparently parallel prophecy of *Dan* 8:8-14) as already fulfilled in the events of the

Emperor Alexander the Great and the Age of Antiochus IV ("Epiphanes"). Most scholars today agree with this - the liberals insiting that the *events precede the prophecy*, and the conservatives insisting that the *prophecy precedes the events*. But Jesus, in the Synoptic Apocalypse, anticipates a further, future, literal fulfillment of these words in the days that will follow His Crucifixion, Burial, Resurrection, and Ascension. (We will deal with this shortly.) Is He, then, denying the conventional understanding that the prophecy regarding the *"abomination of desolation"* is already fulfilled in the events of the Third and Second Centuries B.C.? The view we have developed here regarding the applications of prophecy allows for both understandings, and indeed for many more. Daniel's framework circumscribes and to a considerable degree describes the content of the period 165 B.C. and following; and it no less circumscribes and to a considerable degree describes the content of the period which follows upon Jesus' uttering of His words here in *Matthew* 24:15ff. It is likewise legitimate to hold this original Danielic framework out at mid-distance from the time of its original application (the time of Antiochus IV) to the time of Jesus and through it to see recurring features of the history of the Jews in that period.

Between the "desecration" of the time of Antiochus and Jesus' own time, many features of this Second Century B.C. story were replayed in the First Century B.C. Social and political and cultic issues divided the Jews in the age of the Maccabees (or "Hasmoneans", the royal dynasty established after the overthrow of the Syrians [172-63 B.C.]), just as bitterly as ever before. The failure of the Hasmoneans to maintain national unity tempted outsiders again to intervene. The Romans, by now having built up an empire reaching to the frontiers of Persia, concluded that they could not permit rivals to move into this vacuum. And so again the "Kittim" appeared on the scene, this time moving directly to front and centre when the Roman general Pompey captured the city (63 B.C.), and marched his armies onto the Temple Mount and into the Temple, slaughtering many thousands of its defenders, including its priests. Then Pompey alone went into its very centre, into the Holy of Holies, the "Residence of the LORD".[41]   But Rome, unlike "Epiphanes,", Pompey had no intention of destroying Judaism, which Rome expected in due course to co-opt as another pillar to the spiritual support of its Empire. The day after Pompey entered the Holy of Holies, daily sacrifice resumed.

But over the next century, Roman authorities grew weary of Jewish rigidities about access to the Temple area and complaints about Roman insults, usually unwitting, to their cult.   At intervals, there were popular uprisings against Roman authority. And so from time to time other "abominations" were discovered by Jews and later the Christians in the behaviour of the Roman authorities. In the generation following the Resurrection there seems to have been an escalation of the pace of these events. The Procurator Pilate deliberately outraged the public by bringing images of Caesar into Jerusalem, creating disturbances which were then excuses for bloody suppression.[42] The Emperor Gaius ("Caligula") sent instructions in 40 A.D. to his officers in Judaea to introduce statues of himself into the Temple: "If the Jews refused them," Josephus records, "he [Petronius, the Procurator] was to execute the objectors and enslave all the rest of the population." But Caligula's sudden death prevented the orders from being carried out. The persecutions of Christians by Nero (principally in the city of Rome) during the years 65 to 68 are well known. The Emperor Domitian, in the last decade of the Century, undertook brief but vigorous persecutions of both Christians and Jews; these are likely the persecutions which are in the background to the Book of *Revelation*. All of these events took place before the last of the books of the New Testament were written, and are all apart from the horrible events of the conquest of the city and the destruction of the Temple, in the years 67-70.[43]

Thus, if we hold the framework of Jesus' prophecy out in the middle distance, we see that it circumscribes and to a considerable degree describes a generation of events, whose theme is "abomination" or desecration of the cult of the LORD of Israel and persecution of His people, and to which there is an evident pattern of escalation. The view we have taken here allows as well for the understanding that Jesus is at the same time holding this framework at an *infinite* distance from the plane of life-in-time, so that it circumscribes and in some limited but important detail *describes* the content of the whole of World History, giving us a view of certain definitive features of World History that we will recognize only in the End of Times.

At some point in Daniel's very detailed recital of events preceding and accompanying the days of the "abomination" his voice shifts up several octaves unexpectedly, and he is suddenly describing the End of Times. Christians of equal fidelity, scholarship, and goodwill, differ as to where exactly we should see this happening. Is it at 11:40? Or is it earlier: for instance, at 10:11, so as to include the whole story in the events that belong to the Last Days, thus making all of it future to ourselves? This is one of those extremely volatile issues which it is better not to enter into unless one intends to do it exhaustively. Still, a few points seem clear: There is in these passages the suggestion of a great and ultimate war, apparently embroiling all the powers of the world, including many well outside the orbit of the people of Israel at the time, but with Israel at the centre of the conflict, the object, apparently, of all the accumulated wrath of history (*Dan* 11:40-45). To deal properly with this, we should take into account the similar but much more detailed vision of this ultimate war which is in *Ezekiel* Chaps 38 and 39 - Ezekiel, it should be noted, being a near-contemporary of Daniel. And there are other hints on this same theme in other Prophets.

Large books have been written in the effort to relate all of this to the earlier, much broader-gauged, less-detailed, but more inclusive visions that figure in the Book of *Daniel*: that given to Nebuchadnezzar (in Chapter 2), and those given to Daniel earlier (in Chapters 7 and 8.) Especially provocative (and therefore dangerous) are the few verses that conclude the Book (12:6- 13), spelling out specific arithmetical guidance for reckoning the length of these forthcoming chapters of history. Are those people right who see the arithmetic as applying exclusively to the period before the Advent of Christ, and who try to prove this point by working-out the actual number of years elapsing between Daniel's day and the lifetime of Jesus? [44] But there are others who reckon forward from the day "When the power of the holy people ceases to be dispersed ..." (12:7). But when was (will be) that day! Some of this company started counting with the creation of the State of Israel (in 1948), and others with the recovery of Jerusalem (1967). But this deadline should have passed by now. Others see the day "when the power of the holy people ceases to be dispersed" as still unfulfilled, despite the monumental dimensions of the "ingathering" to the present day; these people watch for signs of a truly completed ingathering of Israel, and have greeted eagerly the ingathering from the Yemen, Syria, Iraq and North Africa, Ethiopia , Russia and the former Soviet Empire. Others say that the Temple must be built first, since this seems to be a precondition for literal fulfillment of v. 11: "From the time when the regular offering is abolished and 'the abomination of desolation' is set up, there shall be an interval of one thousand two hundred and ninety days." My present view is that when we reach the point in World History when we actually and practically *need* these verses, the key will be given to us - just as (we shall see in a moment) the key to *Matthew* 24:15- 16 was given to the Church in the generation that followed His uttering of these words. In the meantime, we have to recognize that much mischief has been done and no doubt today is still being done by people who make authoritative applications of this arithmetic to the history unfolding in front of us, which they may or may not (how can we always be sure?) truly feel in their hearts to be required. But we cling to our earlier consideration: these verses are dangerous because they are about what is real.

We have looked aside from the Synoptic Apocalypse to the Book of *Daniel*, not on a whim, but because Jesus has directed us there in the most explicit terms (*Mt* 24:15f.) It was clearly Jesus' wish for His contemporaries and for us to take this Book and the matters it raises with unqualified seriousness. There are great hazards to the souls of those of both authoritarian and servile temperaments when it comes to the Book of *Daniel* and the other Books and sections of eschatological character of the Bible. Ruinous cultic empires have been reared on these texts. We need only think of "Jehovah's Witnesses." But these risks go with the territory, and do not justify our walking away from them. That option is eliminated by the simple consideration that Jesus directs us to these texts. "This is no idle speculation," said Isaac Newton, "no matter of indifferency, but a duty of the greatest moment."

*　　　　　　*　　　　　　*

Jesus' fullest teaching regarding what remains of World History begins with evocation of a text of Old Testament prophecy, the Book of *Daniel*. He tells His disciples to apply the framework of these prophecies of Daniel to the days ahead, because certain of their themes are about to re-occur. These included the theme of desecration of the Temple and persecution of God's people by the people of the West (the Romans.) When Jesus began to speak to His disciples that day on the Mount of Olives, the disciples were convinced that there was not much left of Israel's history. Jesus had said (from the perspective from which the whole content of time is known) that "your house is forsaken and desolate"

(23:38); and then in effect He doubled the prophecy (24:2-3): "You see all these [stones], do you not? Truly, I say to you, there will not be left here one stone upon another, that will not be thrown down." The Jewish tradition says that when a prophecy is doubled its fulfillment is already being prepared (cf. *Genesis* 41:32).

The disciples heard Him link His coming in triumph with the destruction of the Temple (23:38-9). They had the confidence of their generation that the Temple could not be destroyed, so huge was it, and so weighty were even its smallest individual stones. Herod the Great (37- 4 B.C.) had made a world-class wonder of the Temple, through his massive re-construction and expansion, employing a thousand priests for the actual work, so that the Jews would not accuse him of having built it with unclean hands. The work began in 19 B.C., but was not officially completed until 63 A.D., when Agrippa II was King. In *John* 2:20, the people of Jerusalem Jews say to Jesus: "It has taken forty-six years to build this temple. And you are going to raise it in three days?" (as He seemed to be claiming in v. 19). This exchange seems to fix the dialogue in the year 28 A.D., which most commentators thus accept as the first year of Jesus' ministry. [45] It followed, then, as the night the day, that if the Temple is going to be removed and the place left desolate, it would have to be by God's *superhuman* action. Jesus, they conclude, is speaking of the final act of God in time: the universally-visible Coming of Christ, the final judgement of individuals and nations and the replacement of the Temple of stones by the Temple not made by human hands - all of this the work of Messiah. [46] But, to their interim confusion, Jesus now tells them that they must rethink this current teaching about Messiah and the Temple.

Jesus has been struggling to impress upon them much unwelcome teaching: that He must be captured by the enemies of His own people, tried, and executed; then, after three days in the tomb, He will rise; then will ensue a period of interim before the events of the Last Days. He is not prepared to share with them now - nor will He be willing later, after His resurrection and before His ascension (*Acts* 1:1-9) - the Father's knowledge of the length of this period of interim. The disciples, when they asked this question, no doubt thought that the destruction of the temple would take place at the same time as his coming in glory (the full revelation of His Messsianic power) and the end of the world, with the establishment of his Messianic kingdom (cf. *1.* xxiv. 3.) Therefore Jesus warns them [*Lk* 21: 8-9, & par. *Mt* 24:4-6] not to expect His second advent and the end so soon. They must not allow themselves to be misled by people who profess to be the Christ and announce that the End-time is close at hand. Equally, when they hear of war and insurrections among the nations, they must not be terrified and imagine that the end is already drawing near. All these events will take place, but the end will not come soon. [47]

Matthew 24:6-13 speaks primarily of what awaits the followers of the risen Jesus Christ in the period prior to the destruction of the Temple. In fact, the next four decades were marked by wars, rumours of wars, insurrections within the Empire, and not least in Palestine; there the insurrectionary mood reached a peak in the late sixties, when anti-Roman passions finally provoked the Jewish War, culminating in the terrible slaughter of 70 A.D., and the destruction of the Temple. Likewise, this was a period of spectacular earthquakes (including a severe earthquake in Phrygia, and the eruption of Vesuvius in 61 which is so well known to us today because of the excavations of Pompeii). Likewise, broadscale famine in Italy shook the regimes of Claudius (41-54) and Nero (54-68.) We take nothing away from the predictive significance of these verses with respect to these four decades when we note that wars, rumours of wars, insurrections, famines, and earthquakes have not gone out of the world since, and that there are no doubt items of larger-scale under each of these categories to note in subsequent times, down to and including our own. Nowhere does Jesus say that these four decades are culminating decades, nor that the hazards and horrors of these decades are the ultimate in hazards and horrors. Quite the contrary. He warns the disciples *not* to conclude from the bad news of this period that this is the ultimate bad news, the culminating, record-sweeping and definitive bad news. In these verses, Jesus warned the disciples, who were then still subject to so many misconceptions, that they must not be misled into expecting his second advent, and the final Consummation too soon.

In the "Synoptic Apocalypse" spoken by Jesus, we find at least four distinct frameworks:

(A) a framework which circumscribes and to a considerable degree describes the content of the forty year period from Jesus' ascension (30 A.D. is the best date) to 70 A.D., the year of the destruction of the Temple. Its primary application is seen most clearly in *Mt* 24:4-13.

(B) a narrower framework, which circumscribes and to a considerable degree describes the content of the period 66-70 A.D. Its primary application is most clearly seen in *Mt* 24:15- 26. And,

(C) a framework whose chronological dimensions are specific in God's knowledge, but not in ours - and, during the days before His crucifixion and Resurrection not yet in Jesus' own knowledge [48] - but which circumscribes the whole remainder of World History, until the End of Time.

At different places in this text, we see Jesus holding up one or another of these frameworks in the middle distance, yielding generalizations about the course of time from "now" until 70 A.D., or from "now" until today (the year 2000 A.D.) - or from "now" until the End of Time. It is also possible to understand Him as holding up at an infinite distance from "now" all three of these frameworks simultaneously, given that at the distance of infinity any one will serve to enclose the whole content of time.

The events circumscribed and in part described in the first two frameworks happened later in time, at the normal pace of events happening in time. The historical record shows that everything said here proved to be sufficiently clear that the Christian community, remembering these very words of Jesus, interpreted the signs correctly, and withdrew from Jerusalem deliberately, without haste or panic, reassembling across the Jordan in Pella, and thereby escaping participation in the events circumscribed and in part described in framework B. His words were: "So when you see the desolating sacrilege spoken of by the prophet Daniel, standing in the holy place (let the reader understand), then let those who are in Judaea flee to the mountains ... " (*Mt* 24:15-16.) The Church historian, Eusebius (263-339), born in Palestine, and eventually the Bishop of Caesarea, describes how the Church did in fact watch for these political and military signs of which Jesus spoke, and saw them realized in the movement of Roman armies to quell popular disturbances beginning in 67 A.D. Eusebius also speaks of an "oracle, given by revelation to acceptable persons, which ordered them to leave the City before the war began and to settle in a town in Peraea called Pella." [49] In this way, they fulfilled the prophetic advice of *Mt* 24:15-16.

In the "Introduction" to his translation of Josephus, *The Jewish War*, G.A. Williamson takes note of the remarkable correspondence between Jesus' description in *Mt* 24 and actual features of the Roman siege and subsequent destruction of the Temple, as described by Josephus:

> It was the startling accuracy of our Lord's warning that led critics of a generation ago, committed to the principle that every prophecy is written after the event - a principle of which there is not a shred of justification in science, philosophy, or experience - to allege that the great prophecies recorded by Matthew, Mark, and Luke were borrowed from later works of apocalyptic or eschatology and "put

into Christ's mouth". These critics overlooked several facts. Leaving out of count the transparent honesty of the gospel writers, we notice that while these later works were concerned with the end of the world, Christ was obviously thinking much more about events which His own generation was to witness. The disciples, Matthew tells us, had asked Him a double question - about the destruction of the Temple and about His own final coming - and He gave them a double answer, the first part of which most vividly foretold the occurrences destined to be so fully described by Josephus. He made it clear to his audience how the imminence of those occurrences was to be recognized, and instructed them what they were to do when the warning signs were observed. This the Christians remembered and carried out: before the City was encompassed by its enemies they fled to Pella and so escaped the general destruction. It is hard to account for this escape if the prophecy was written after the event. [50]

Not spectacular supernatural signs but political signs - political signs of a particularly conspicuous sort (*"let the reader understand"*) [51] but nonetheless entirely belonging to the normal category of political events - will be the signs of the imminent destruction of the Temple. "And now," writes Geldenhuys, "at last [*Mt* 24:15-20] Jesus tells them of the sign which is to indicate that the destruction of the city and the temple is close at hand. It will be something quite different from His second advent. Thus the destruction of Jerusalem will *not* be preceded by the revelation of his messianic glory. By no means, for when the city begins to be threatened by earthly armies ... the faithful must know that its destruction at the hands of those armies is at hand." [52]

When they see these signs, they must flee immediately from Jerusalem, thereby escaping the consequences of the two fatal alternatives: (i) believing that political events cannot be as bad as they seem, and will be resolved as always before, with the antagonists crawling down from their extreme positions; or (ii) believing that God would intervene in supernatural way precisely as things get utterly hopeless. The first of these was the error of the secularists;

the second was the error of the religious enthusiasts, who tragically captured the whole population of the city within the walls with their visions of Messianic rescue. [53]

Held up at middle distance, both frameworks yield generalizations about the long course of World History. But this was not their *primary* application. And had the Early Church for a moment believed that generalization about the course of World History was the primary purpose for which they had been given, the Church would have been destroyed. It is no less true for us: that if we deny the force of these prophecies as foreknowledge which was in fact vindicated in *specific historical events* (the events of 66-70 A.D.) then we will be better off passing up the possible applied uses of these words: i.e., their capacity to yield generalizations about the long haul of history.

Jesus is telling us to apply the framework of these prophecies to the days ahead of us, notwithstanding that we have seen their realization already in the events of the period culminating in 70 A.D. Simultaneously, He is holding up the framework of these prophecies in the middle distance, between His days and the Days of the End, to give us generalized truths about the course of history to come. In the same gesture, He is as well holding up these frameworks at an *infinite* distance from the plane of life-in-time to allow us to see some of How it All Ends.

We see what we are allowed to see here through these specific frameworks. Had we been given other frameworks, we would see other truths about the whole course of time and How it All Ends. Elsewhere in Scripture, both Old and New, we are given other such frameworks. *Daniel* 11 and 12, just considered, is one such. *Ezekiel* 38 and 39 is another. And in the New Testament there are eschatological passages in certain of the Apostles' letters (notably, in *I Corinthians*, in I and *II Thessalonians*, and *II Peter*). And of course there is the Apocalypse of John (*Revelation*).

We have to understand these prophetic frameworks of Jesus in the same light as those of Isaiah, already discussed. There (pp. 133-134) we said that the framework of *Isaiah* 7 and 8, applied directly to the plane of life-in-time, yields a specific content of history: the specific events of about a three year period, coinciding with the conception, birth, and growth to the first stages of understanding, of a Child-life, the life of "Immanuel." Held at an infinite distance from the plane of life-in-time, the same framework encloses a theme that embraces the whole content of World History: namely, the conception, birth and the childhood of the Saviour. The Church has always claimed that that framework, held up at an infinite distance from the plane of life-in-time, yields the eternal meaning of the nativity of Jesus of Nazareth.

In precisely the same way, what I have called frameworks A and B of the Synoptic Apocalypse, held at an infinite distance from the plane of life-in-time, display certain definitive features of the whole content of World History. As there are definitive themes in the Child/Immanuel framework of *Isaiah* 7 and 8 - anticipating the history of the Nativity of Jesus of Nazareth, whose effects will govern the remainder of World History to the End of Time - so in these frameworks of Jesus' apocalyptic message there are anticipations of things to be realized definitively in World History, and which will govern the remainder of World History, to the end of time. For example: *Matthew* 24:6 speaks of "wars and rumours of wars", "famines and earthquakes," all of which there were in more than normal proportions in the decades immediately following the uttering of these words. [54] But even so what is pictured here seems to belong to a much vaster canvas than merely that of the years from roughly 30 A.D. (when, most historians would say, Jesus spoke these words) to 70 A.D., when the destruction of the Temple was completed - or, for that matter, for the period extended to 131-5 A.D., the years of the Bar

Kokhba revolt which replayed the themes of popular uprising again the Roman authority, the appearance of a false Messiah, the cruel slaughter of many thousands, and the final levelling of the Temple Mount, followed by the imposition of a pagan temple on the site. In the next verses (24:8f), it is as though everything has been taken up an octave - and then several further octaves, to encompass generalizations about the whole span of history to its conclusion. This culminates in verse 22, where He is clearly talking about the Last Days.

Beginning with verse 23, it no longer seems possible to continue to see the *primary* application of these words in the period 30 A.D. to 135 A.D. We must hold the framework out to a hypothetically infinite distance - for something radically new has come into the picture: *the sun will be darkened, and the moon will not give its light* (v. 29). But lest we think that something momentary is meant (an eclipse, for example), we are then told that *the stars will fall from heaven and the powers of heaven will be shaken* (v. 30).

In the centuries that followed, the Bishops and theologians of the Church tried the experiment of holding these frameworks imaginatively at an infinite distance from the plane of life-in-time, and eventually incorporated what they could see most clearly into the Creed: Jesus Christ will return, in real historical time, to judge the quick and the dead. Theologians, amateur and certified, have seen other themes: a definitive, global, cataclysmic war in the End of Times; the rescue (rapture) of the Church prior to this cataclysm; and other themes that do not have standing within the Creed, but are widely embraced by people of faith and Biblical learning. The fullest of the clues, and the one which has provided the missionary motive for centuries, is the statement that "this gospel of the kingdom will be preached throughout the whole world, as a testimony to all nations; and then the end will come" (*Mt* 24:14.)

CHAPTER SIX: The Restoration of Israel.

> In the last day there will appear in full view the
> mountain of the Lord, prepared on the summit of the mountains,
> and lifted up above the hills; and all the nations will come to it,
> and many nations will enter and say: "Come, let us go up to the
> mountain of God, and go into the house of the God of Jacob;
> and he will announce to us his way, and we will start upon it."
> For the Law will issue out of Sion, and The Word of the Lord
> from Jerusalem [*Isaiah* 2:2].

The modern mind hates to be surprised.

    - Abraham J. Heschel.

Israel's Re-appearance in the Company of Nations.

The first mention of the name "Israel" occurring in an extra-Biblical document is on a list of the enemies of the Pharoah Meneptah some thirty-two centuries ago. The reference reads in full: "*Israel is no more.*" Yet today, there is in the world in the world only one nation which speaks the same language, practises the same religion, and occupies the same portion of the world's surface that it did when that document came into the world. And that is Israel, the nation which is addressed by that same name forty centuries ago, and declared to be "no more." [55]

The State of Israel declared its existence as a modern nation-state of May 14, 1948, responding to a commitment made to the Jewish people of the world by two-thirds of the membership of the newly-created United Nations on November 29, 1947. It is an awesome thought that of all the names of the nations we would need to tell the story of how the State of Israel was restored in consequence of the decision of 1947-1948 (the United States of America, the Soviet Union, Britain, the British Commonwealth and Empire, France, China, India - even Canada!), not one was in the world when the name "Israel" first appeared in political reports some forty centuries ago. Indeed, many centuries would roll by before any of these proper names would appear in the world. For that matter, many centuries would roll by before any of the languages in which the debate about Israel's right to exist was conducted in those days - not excluding *English*, the language in which this argument is being offered - would begin to take shape.

A few centuries went by, and then the Empire of the Pharoahs was *no more*. Indeed, all of the nations which appear on Meneptah's list - some of which subsequently increased in strength and became great empires themselves - have disappeared. None of the languages spoken by any of the nations on that list is still alive as a spoken or literary language in the world. Whether or not one attaches theological meaning to any part of this story, this is still a true story, and should command respect, or at least cause one to pause.

*   *   *

In the "Prologue" to his *A History of the Jews*, [56] Paul Johnson reviews his motives in undertaking such a book. First of all, he tells us that in writing his *A History of Christianity* (1976), he had become aware of "the magnitude of the debt Christianity owes to Judaism," and had subsequently sought out "an opportunity ... to write about the people who had given birth to my faith." Secondly, there was the excitement and the challenge posed by the sheer span of Jewish history: for, as we have already had reason to consider, there is no other branch of historiography that takes one back so far, and provides anything like its abundant material for continuous narrative forward in time. Furthermore: the History of the Jews encompasses not only vast tracts of time, but also huge areas of space: for the unique story of the scattering of the Jews provides leads into the stories of virtually all of the histories of civilized communities in all corners of the globe. As Johnson describes it, "The Jews have penetrated many societies and left their mark on all of them. Writing a history of the Jews is almost like writing a history of the world, but from a highly peculiar angle of vision. It is world history seen from the viewpoint of a learned and intelligent victim."

But one motive came to outmatch all of these:

> Finally the book gave me the chance to reconsider objectively, in the light of a study covering nearly 4,000 years, the most intractable of all human questions: what are we on earth for? Is history merely a series of events whose sum is meaningless? ... Is there a providential plan of which we are, however humbly, the agents? No people has ever insisted more firmly than the Jews that history has a purpose and humanity a destiny. At a very early stage in their collective existence they believed they had detected a divine scheme for the human race, of which their own society was to be the pilot. They worked out their role in immense detail. They clung to it with heroic persistence in the face of savage suffering. Many of them believe it still. Others transmuted it into Promethean endeavours to raise our condition by purely human means. The Jewish vision became the prototype for many similar grand designs for humanity, both divine and man-made. The Jews, therefore, stand right at the centre of the perennial attempt to give human life the dignity of a purpose.

Through the main body of the book, these reflections are set aside, even though there are frequent hints that Johnson has not lost sight of them. Then, in the "Epilogue," he returns to them: "In his *Antiquities of the Jews*, Josephus describes Abraham as 'a man of great sagacity' who had 'higher notions of virtue than others of this time.' He therefore 'determined to change completely the views which all then had about God.' One way of summing up 4,000 years of Jewish history is to ask ourselves what would have happened to the human race if Abraham had not been a man of great sagacity, or if he had stayed in Ur and kept his higher notions to himself, and no specific Jewish people had come into being." [57]

The line of thought which Johnson opens up at this point is reckless, and threatens to jeopardize all the good that he has done by drawing his readers' attention to this largest of possible historical visions. It is pointless to pretend that there is somewhere in possibility a world in which Abraham does not chose to obey God. It is irresponsible, and puts under radical threat the whole of what we claim on behalf of the meaning of Abraham's decision, to pretend that we can hold up for study some parallel human history of the imagination where there is an Abraham who decided differently. The whole possibility of telling the whole human story as a single story, having a linear direction and accumulating meanings and occurring entirely upon the ground of this life-in-time, follows *exclusively* from the exercise of tracing the consequences of that decision. Johnson is tempting us here into the original Greek-philosophical trap of pretending to learn about the meaning of history by comparing *what was* to *what might alternatively have been*. When we play these games, we make philosophy and science the measure of meaning, and we reduce history's authority to its usefulness in illustrating what philosophy and science know with authority.

Furthermore: we miss the central claim of our Scripture when we reduce

Abraham's significance to that of a "man of ideas!" Talking in this way of Abraham's "notions," of "Jewish insights" and "conceptual discoveries," and, a little further on, of how "the Jews taught us how to rationalize the unknown" and thus were able to "give us monotheism" - this sort of talk amounts to throwing away with the left hand what Paul Johnson has just offered us with the right: the vision of the possibility of giving order to the story of mankind by tracing the way of the Jews through time and space. It misses the whole point of what Scripture says about Abraham *and about us* if we picture Abraham *thinking his way to the idea of One God*. He was confronted by the Living God Who demanded a decision of him. In this light, Martin Buber said that whereas ever since Plato, philosophers see; ever since Moses, Jews hear.[58]

So, while it is true that Jews have accomplished the great works of thought which Johnson rightly dwells upon; and while it is true that these great works of thought have had the incalculable impact upon the course of social, economic, political, religious and intellectual history that Johnson describes; and while these have to be weighed up and considered as the contribution of the Jews to World History – these matters do not amount to the meaning of the History of the Jews. Nor does it come anywhere near exhausting the meaning of the History of the Jews to say that History has proved to be a great "paradigm," even the most powerful of paradigms, of all other histories: "We all want to build Jerusalem. We all drift back towards the Cities of the Plain. It seems to be the role of the Jews to focus and dramatize these common experiences of mankind, and to turn their particular fate into a universal moral." But then, as if suddenly alert to the secular drift of his own thought, Johnson pulls back: " But if the Jews have this role, who wrote it for them?"

Precisely! Even if we settle for the idea that the History of the Jews only serves as a paradigm, we are already skirting the edge of Purpose. No sooner is that rhetorical question out of the box, than Johnson stuffs it back again:

"Historians should beware of seeking providential patterns in events. They are all too easily found, for we are credulous creatures, born to believe, and equipped with powerful imaginations which readily produce and rearrange data to suit any transcendental scheme." If this is merely a reminder that, in the search for historical fact, we must suspend theological or philosophical reflection, no responsible Christian historian will quarrel with these words. But this is a red herring. It is not true that the best way to equip oneself for historical study is to rigorously doubt all possibility of transcendent meaning. On the contrary: the energies that are necessary for pressing on with objective discovery of fact always trace to some kind of faith that the whole story adds up to something meaningful. Momentarily embarrassed by this reality, Johnson settles for suggesting that among *all the other* items of evidence we collect as historians, we must also "take into account ... those which are or appear to be metaphysical." By "metaphysical," Johnson apparently means *not material*. The and the example he gives of this class of evidence is the confidence of the Jews that they would persist until the end of history. This, he suggests - and who would want to deny it? - is an inseparable part of the meaning of the story of the Jews: " If the earliest Jews were able to survey with us, the history of their progeny, they would find nothing surprising in it. They always knew that Jewish society was appointed to be a pilot-project for the entire human race .... That Jews should over the millennia attract such unparalleled, indeed inexplicable, hatred would be regrettable but only to be expected. Above all, that Jews should still survive, when all those other ancient people were transmuted or vanished into the oubliettes of history, was wholly predictable."

"Predictable," by what logic? "Predictable," perhaps, *to them* - that is, to Jewish faith. But the fact of the Jews' survival, precisely because we find it to be "unparalleled" and "inexplicable" - in short, unique - cannot be said to illustrate any law of history. The whole point is that this story contradicts the laws, and thus the possibilities of "prediction." The ancient Jews knew what no other knowledge could or can detect: that they alone would survive out of the ancient chapters of World History; and furthermore, that only because of the story of their survival - and only on that ground - would it prove possible for all other nations to tell the whole story of mankind as a single story, with accumulating meaning, as our civilization has done for centuries. The *objective* point is that all the other ancient people believed, too, that they would live forever; but forces which every student of history quickly discovers to be recurring, and which theorists of history cherish as "laws", swept them all away. Not so the Jews. " Providence [the ancient Jews would have said] decreed it [their unique survival] and the Jews obeyed. The historian may say: there is no such thing as providence. Possibly not. But human confidence in such an historical dynamic, if it is strong enough, is a force in itself, which pushes on the hinge of events and moves them. The Jews believed they were a special people with such unanimity and passion, and over so long a span, that they became one. They did indeed have a role because they wrote it for themselves. Therein, perhaps, lies the key to their story." [59]

Paul Johnson, a man of sturdy Christian faith, believes (rightly) in the scholarly obligation to divide between matters of faith and matters of empirical observation. But here he draws the line in the wrong place. By concluding on this limp anti-climax - They wrote the role for themselves! - Johnson proves disloyal to the vision of World History directed by another Purpose than the sum-total of all the role-writing and all the role-playing that clearly does go on in it. The persistence of the Jews and of Judaism, the very possibility that World History can be ordered on the theme of the origins, the gathering, and the scattering, and now in our days the re-gathering of the Jews - all of this cries out for explanation. And the explanation must, by logic, be "metaphysical," in the correct philosophical sense, if we are to say that the story is "unparalleled" and (by the ordinary, discoverable "laws" of history) "inexplicable" in plain terms, unique. To recast what is "metaphysical" in this story as that which the Jews (or rather some of them) persuaded themselves to believe, mocks the first premise of faith. Believers should not settle for this trivialization of what is "metaphysical" - which is, after all, in the spirit of Feuerbach and the philosophical deniers of transcendence, and is not a fit usage for believers.

Elsewhere in the book, and showing greater consistency than in his "Epilogue," Johnson does in fact boldly entertain transcendent possibilities of understanding the History of the Jews. In the sections where he describes the origins and development of the American Jewish community, he expresses directly his sense of wonder at the evident purposefulness of this story: "It was as though history was slowing solving a great jigsaw puzzle, slipping the pieces into their places one after another." [60] He marvels at the timing that resulted from the evacuation of a great portion of Central European Jewry (mainly from the Austro-Hungarian and the Russian Empires) to America, following the pograms of the 1880's. (The descendants of those who remained were nearly all destroyed in the Holocaust.) He reviews the exceptional social, economic and religious circumstances in the American historical setting which nourished the self-esteem and the political confidence of the American Jews. And behind that peculiar story, he tells us, is an equally odd-shaped "piece of the puzzle" : this is the exceptional enthusiasm for the restoration of the Jews to Zion which existed in the English-speaking world, especially among those whose philosophy was rooted in historic Puritanism.

> We have used the image of the jigsaw puzzle to show how each necessary piece was slotted into place. As we have seen, the great eastern massacres of 1648 led to the return of a Jewish community

to England, and so to America, this in time producing the most influential Jewry in the world, an indispensable part of the geopolitical context in which Israel could be created. Again, the massacres of 1881 [in Poland, Ukraine, and Russia] set in motion a whole series of events ending towards the same end. The immigration they produced was the background to the Dreyfus outrage, which led directly to Herzl's creation of modern Zionism. The movement of Jews set in motion by Russian oppression created the pattern of tension from which, in 1917, the Balfour Declaration emerged and the League of Nations Palestine mandate was set up to implement it. Hitler's persecution of the Jews was the last in the series of catastrophes which helped to make the Zionist state. [61]

The metaphor of the jigsaw puzzle is a rather good one. Yet it is simply incompatible with the metaphor which appears in the last sentences of the book (already quoted), - where the Jews are seen as (somehow) *writing their own role* for themselves. There is no possibility of mixing and matching elements of the two metaphors If we are ready to take the risks that go with the metaphor of the jigsaw puzzle, we hold in our hands the only full and sufficient theory of history that the world has ever produced.

There is no incompatibility between holding a theological view of history's meaning and the work of assiduous and honorable and objective historical research. In fact, historically the two habits of mind have always flourished best in tandem. It was Christian historians (the pious *erudits* whom Voltaire so despised) who established the modern criteria in these matters. Their rightful heir was Leopold von Ranke, who spoke of his work as studying "the tracks of God." An eminent modern historian of the classical world, Marcus Finley speaks of the "persistent misconception" about Ranke which is to be found in all the textbooks on Philosophy of History: in such textbooks, he says, Ranke is always presented "as the 'father of scientific history', the model historian who was determined to hold strictly to the facts of history, 'to preach no sermon' [citing Georg Iggers, *The German Conception of History.*] Did

the pedants who reduced Ranke's historiography to such 'soulless positivism'
ever read him, one wonders, or were they content with parroting *wie es
eigentlich gewesen*? Behind that gross misunderstanding there of course lay
the long familiar hankering of the academic humanist for the certainties of the
natural sciences. One sympathizes with that ... but complete honesty, respect for
critical evaluation of evidence, are only necessary conditions for history-writing
as for science; they are not sufficient conditions for either." [62]

It is an evasion of responsibility to try to soften the point of all of this by
saying, as Johnson does, that it was as though history was solving a great
jigsaw puzzle. It is not *as though* anything. It is not history -- nor is it History,
nor even HISTORY) that is doing its own solving. History is the puzzle. The
solving, obviously, has to be going on above the puzzle. It is only because post-
Christian thought is embarrassed by straight God-talk that Christians borrow
this half-way talk.

The Meaning of the Restoration of Israel.

> He will gather you again from all the countries to which he has
> scattered you. Even though he were to banish you to the four
> corners of the world, the LORD your God will gather you from
> there, from there he will fetch you home. The LORD your God
> will bring you into the land which your forefathers occupied, and
> you will occupy it again (*Deuteronomy* 30:3-5 [NEB]).

The Restoration of Israel is embedded in the pattern of the puzzle
which is History. There have always been faithful Jews and faithful Christians
for whom this is the key to History. The "metaphysical" thing about World
History is not that *some people have always believed* that the History of the Jews
was subject to another Law than the laws of science and philosophy, but

rather that *objectively* World History has been impossible to recite on any other ground than as the outcome of the decision of Abraham, the Father of the Jews. Thus, the "metaphysical" fact is also an objective fact. The restoration of Israel follows as the consequence of the accumulating effects of Abraham's decision. These consequences occur entirely on the plane of this life-in-time. They can be traced in a purely descriptive, causal way, from the beginning to the present.

All larger considerations aside, the Christian's sense for the seriousness of what happens in history requires him to regard the re-establishment of the State of Israel as a proof that the God of our faith is the Lord of History. We are assured by the philosophers that none of the traditional scholars' Proofs of God (the Common Consent Proof, the Ontological Proof, the Moral Proof, the Teleological Proof, and the others which I have forgotten) can *compel* consent. Hence, when we say that the objective fact of the Restoration of Israel belongs in the company of Proofs of the Existence of God, we do not pretend to say that this is a compelling proof. Historical evidence, by its specially vulnerable nature, is never compelling. With these caveats in place, we say that *the Restoration of the State of Israel in our own time is the best proof of the Sovereignty of the God of History*, proof of history's authority to tell us the largest things about life.

While there have always been Christian Zionists, there have likewise also always been Christian anti-Zionists. For these latter, as for anti-Zionist Jews, there was always the sense that it was disloyal to the promises of Scripture to attempt to make of the Jews a nation like other nations. To theologically-orthodox Christians, this sounded like denying that the Second Covenant had replaced the First. To theologically-liberal Christians and theologically-liberal Jews, it sounded like denying the *universality* of the message of Judaism. To theologically-orthodox Jews it sounded like a denial of confidence that Messiah Himself would bring the Jews home and found their Kingdom.

The case of Karl Barth will help to make this point. It was in 1941-2 that this most eminent of Twentieth Century Protestant theologians reached the point in his *Church Dogmatics*, his life-work, where he must address the question of "Israel and the Church." This he did in the section #34: "The Election of the Community". [63] The argument is developed in Barth's characteristically fulsome way; but here is a key passage:

> If Israel were obedient to its election, its special witness to the passing of the old man and his world, taken up into the confession of the whole community of God's coming kingdom, would supplement and harmonize with the Church's witness of hope founded on the resurrection of Jesus Christ ... [But Israel] resists the gracious passing from which alone it could now emerge alive, but from which it may really emerge alive. It takes a rigid stand on a carnal loyalty to itself and on a carnal hope [i.e., nationhood] corresponding to this loyalty ... If Israel wills and does what is intrinsically impossible this is in the truest sense of the word its own affair. In so doing it condemns itself and burdens and troubles itself ... Old things have passed away. All things are become new ... [Refusing, in its unbelief of the Christian message, to see this,] It must be the personification of a half- venerable, half-gruesome relic, of a miraculously preserved antique, of human whimsicality. It must now live among the nations the patterns of a historical life which has absolutely no future - but without having its appointed time like the other nations, being then allowed to take its leave and be merged in others. In this way it punishes itself. In this way it disrupts the community of God. [64]

These severe words (spoken from neutral Switzerland in 1941-1942) express Barth's objection to all the talk going on around him in those days about the right and the necessity of the Jews' establishing a State for their Nation in Palestine. His opposition is strictly theological, deriving from rigorous defense of Christian faith as the New Covenant replacing the Old. But in our time, *it has come about: Israel has been restored.* In retrospect, it is possible to trace cause and effect - as, for example, Paul Johnson does brilliantly (as we have seen); and it is possible then to say that there is so much about the way that circumstances came together that one must think of it all as a great jigsaw puzzle being "worked out." In future, whatever else may befall Israel or any other nation, it will be impossible to read Scripture without the knowledge that Israel was restored, in the form and character of a nation-state, on May 14, 1948.

In his *Israel: An Echo of Eternity*, Abraham Heschel puts the matter in these challenging terms: "The State of Israel is a surprise, yet the modern mind hates to be surprised. Never before has a nation been restored to its ancient hearth after a lapse of 1,897 years. This extraordinary aspect is bound to carry some shock to the conventional mind, to be a scandal to the mediocre mind and a foolishness to the positivists. It requires some reordering of some notions ... Zion rebuilt becomes a harbinger of a new understanding, of how history is intertwined with mystery .... It is an accord of divine promise and human achievment." [65] In the last few months before his death on December 9, 1968, Karl Barth, "surprised" by the current unfolding of events, had the grace to reconsider his thinking about the meaning of the State of Israel. After the Six Day War of June, 1967, Barth still felt (according to his biographer) that "it was necessary to make a distinction between one's political assessment of the situation and the biblical view of the people of Israel. Of course the foundation of the State of Israel was not to be seen as an analogy to the conquest under Joshua and thus as a sign that God cannot let his people be defeated. 'Yet [he said] we can read in the newspapers: "God keeps his promise." ' " [66]

The perdurance of "Israel" is an absolute refutation of all the generalizations that can be drawn from the most conscientious search of the record of History. Arnold Toynbee, who tried hardest of all our contemporaries to search with the finest of fine-tooth combs the materials of history and shape them into *laws,* agonized about this point - and ended up in a rage. Determined not to admit that Israel had emerged as the only survivor of the ancient Mesopotamian civilizations, and equally determined to "classify" it, he concluded that it was a "Syriac fossil." [67] We take a different view: that the re-establishment of the State of Israel in our own time is an utterly unparalleled event in World History. It is a proof that "God keeps his promise," in this case, the particular promise that we first see stated in *Deuteronomy* 30, and which recurs throughout Old Testament Scripture. Writing in the early 1940's, Barth spoke of "the patterns of historical life" which, as he rightly put it, amount to a rule that nations "have their appointed time," that they "leave" or "merge into others." That is indeed what all the most thorough study of history shows. This same logic bound the earliest Christian theorists of History (culminating in Augustine) to the conclusion that the "earthly Jerusalem" had passed away forever, and that all the promises to her by the Jewish God now belong to the Church (the "spiritual Jerusalem") or to the Life to Come (the "heavenly Jerusalem.") With respect to the question of the historical meaning of "Israel," the Church was, prior to 1948, in a position like that of the earliest generation of the Church with respect to the question of the future of the Temple. When the political and military events of 67-70 A.D. began to unfold, the Church saw in them a kind of fulfillment that it had not anticipated. But the point is that when it saw these events, it reviewed the words that it had been given by Jesus (*Matthew* 23 and 24, and parallels), and it acted. The phrase "the abomination of desolation," and the language about no stone being left upon another - all this now was seen to have specific reference in the events of this life-in-time, in the actions of the Roman authorities and of the priests and the popular agitators. When Jerusalem was invested by the Romans, the Christians fled to Pella, thereby escaping the mass death and destruction that overcome the Jews who refused to believe that God would permit the temple to fall. Similarly: in the light of the facts of history in our own time - the creation of the State of Israel in 1948, the re-capture of Jerusalem, Judea and Samaria in 1967 - the words "Israel" and "Jerusalem" and "Zion" now have possibilities of application that could not be seen until the present generation. In the light of the restoration of Israel, the Lord of History has demonstrated History's right to contradict what philosophy thinks that it knows.

*   *   *

Chapter Seven: Beyond Chaos: A Calm Look At How It All Ends.

The Triumph of Chaos: A Look at Secular Eschatology.

Every day, people everywhere are becoming more obssessed with dark possibilities of calamity and chaos. A recently published popular work of geography introduces a survey of present geographical knowledge with these chilling words:

> PLANET EARTH.
> It is wholly remarkable that our planet is habitable at all. A few miles beneath our feet, a nuclear-powered inferno rages. Another impact with a mile-wide meteor, and a new ice age might ensue. A little closer to the sun, or a slower spin, or a few percentage points more of oxygen in the atmosphere, and all living things would burn to ash. [68]

Hitherto unexpected hazards to the continuing of the earth are announced every day in the newspaper. In recent days, these have developed at a geometric rate, reaching an apparent crescendo some months ago in a universal obsession with possibilities of doom entailed in the so-called Y2K-problem, which was foreseen as a sort of massive aneurism within the *noosphere*, the universal information system, the thinking membrane which humans have put in place around the biosphere (the living layer.) As the end of 1999 approached, some were speaking of the end of Civilization As We Know It (TEOCAWKI.) How ironical it seemed that a trivial misjudgement, a momentary lapse of imagination (the failure to foresee the need for four-digits to register the date after the end of the Twentieth Century) might be about to bring down the the whole Faustian enterprise called Global Information. Perversely, these prognostications of doom habitually borrowed upon the vocabulary of Christian Scripture. Words like "millennium" and "apolcalyptic" are words of Hope in Christian Scripture - something one would never guess from their use in the titles of the several deranged television series which are the leading-items in nightime television.

In the course of a single generation, since Hiroshima, a revolutionary and irreversible change has come over the morale of the world. The world now lives with the truth that the religious mind has always known: the truth that in an instant of time, and possibly without warning, everything that is real could disappear into nothingness. Various surveys show that the possibility of annihilation of our world through nuclear war or accident is the greatest fear of young people. The fact that the world now has this knowledge, and that this knowledge is moving at an accelerating rate from the furthest to the nearest reaches of awareness in people's minds, should be the governing consideration in the Church's present dealings with the world.

During the 1970s and 1980s, the two "Superpowers" and their allies agreed to reduce reduce nuclear arsenals and delivery systems, dramatically reducing, it seemed, the probability of annihilation of our world through nuclear war. The end of the Cold War and the collapse of the Soviet Empire momentarily lessened people's fear of possible nuclear war. Soon, however, the old spirit of fear returned, as several of the successor states of the U.S.S.R. took custody of the still-abundant stockpiles. Soon political commentators were warning us that a black market had sprung up for the purpose of selling materials, technology, and ever the services of unemployed Soviet scientists and engineers to middle and even middling powers - "rogue states," whose internal politics have been notably violent, whose leaders are committed to policies of revenge against other states or against various imagined global enemies. In recent years, India and Pakiston have announced their graduation to the ranks of the nuclear powers. Israel is presumed to be a nuclear power. North Korea and Iran and any number of others are preparing to qualify for inclusion in that company. In May of 1999, we learned that the People's Republic of China had infiltrated all the major centers of military and high-technology research, and had acquired all the knowledge necessary to bring it quickly into the same league with the United States as a nuclear power. Furthermore, China was relaying this purloined knowledge and production to every regime that could meet its bargain prices.

At the same time, earnest debate rages over whether other forces are not more lethal than nuclear weapons and the risks which attend the production of nuclear industrial power. Certain natural processes (most, but not all, aggravated by human willfulness, gluttony, or neglect) are, some say, working invincibly towards global catastrophe. The catalogue of these processes is long, and to it some researcher adds another item every day:

* Food resources are depleting, and in danger of ultimately failing, owing to over-production and exhaustion of soils, the advance of deserts, the

disappearance of wetlands, the effects of wars, foreign and domestic, the pollution by industrial and human wastes of rivers, lakes, and the ocean itself.

* Several irreversible processes are believed to be assaulting the ozone layer, which alone protects us from lethal bombardment of solar rays.

* The magnetic field is being reversed, a process that we can measure with absolute accuracy, but are powerless to affect. At some point (probably the mid-Twenty Second Century) a realignment of the poles will take place abruptly; the magnetic field, which normally protects us from solar radioactivity will be neutralized, and world-wide cataclysm will ensue.

* A quantum leap in the global population of termites, accompanied by a corresponding increase in the prevalence of termite flatulence, threatens to blow away altogether the ozone layer. [69]

The modern-scientific mind now "knows" that the end of all things is imminent. Who is to contradict it? Science projects these futuristic "probabilities" by means of scientific reasoning. There is the same mix of hypothesis/experiment, deduction/induction, prognosis/diagnosis in these statements as in the classic statements upon which the scientific method was built. It knows these future meanings with the same mind that it knows the chemistry of glucose. This is the same mind we have come to depend upon for our modern medicine, the building of our bridges, our conquest of space, the breathtaking accomplishments in transportation and communication, and the discovery of the previously secret processes that take place within the molecule and the gene cells. This mind tells us that chaos underlies everything: man-made structures, and the given structures of this natural world in all its reaches, from the sub-molecular to the cosmic. Contrary to the vision of modern sciene in its earliest hours, current textbooks describe sub-atomic reality as "a view of chaos beneath order - or, what is the same thing, of order imposed upon a deeper and more fundamental chaos." [70] Reason, logic, arithmetic, cellular chemistry, astronomical physics, political science, economics - all point in the same direction.

There have been many waves of apocalyptic mania in the past. The absolutely unique features about this present wave derives from the absolutely unique feature, the *differentia specifica*, of our modern western culture: namely, that it is *scientific*. All previous cultures (including the pre-modern European one) looked to supernatural faith as the primary source of meaning. As a result, the bad news as well as the good news came from religious reflection. The religious mind has always known that at every moment in time and at every point of the scale of reality chaos is the built-in probability. Order is redeemed out of the ostensibly (objectively) overwhelming tendency to chaos in every realm of life in every moment of time. This is true in the world of human affairs and in the world of sub-molecular dynamics, and in "worlds" both "beneath" and "above" this scale.

The imminent end of all things in fire stands before the world today as an insight of the modern-scientific mind! *Cogito ergo sum.* To every action there is always opposed an equal reaction. $E = mc2$. The end is near.

The current "discoveries" and "projections" of science do not add anything to the basic Christian understanding of the end of all things. This knowledge is based on trust in statements of the Creator-God to be found in His infallible Word, to which we go for the truth about our present situation and about the whole pattern of History. Christians ought not to be impressed by the fact that the descriptive sciences and the academic disciplines of the modern mind now see the advancing probability of annihilation of everything.

This is not a new line of speculation for Christians. Furthermore, Christians do not believe that, in the most real sense, this outcome is more "probable" in the year 2000 - when nuclear weapons are mounted on tens of thousands of combat-ready weapons, governed by computer "programs" increasingly prey to cyberterrorism, than it was in the day when flint-tipped spears were the ultimate weapon.

God has by stages disclosed to scientific discovery that along all the paths of natural dynamics in the cosmos there is a striving towards chaos. This is the warp of reality. There is no *tendency to order* in reality! Along the weft of reality, God is picking up, canceling-out, bringing together, shaping life out of death-tending chaos. Scripture says that He does this out of "patience" - for the purpose of giving us time to turn to Him; time in which to be remade for a new beginning in "new heavens and a new earth."

The last pages of Christian Scripture are taken up with this always-imminent inevitability that the modern mind is just now "discovering." The last book of the Christian canon outlines "the revelation [*apokalypse*] given by God to Jesus Christ," and then conveyed by Jesus to "his servant John" (possibly the ranking survivor among Christ's disciples, in his extreme old age), by means of which John was given to understand some features of the historical process as it tended to the end of time. The "Pastoral Epistles" (the penultimate section of the Christian Bible) bristle with speculations about the end of all things and with exhortations on the urgency of addressing this reality. The message is perhaps best summed-up in these words of Peter:

> [T]he day of the Lord will come as a thief in the night, in which the heavens will pass away with a great noise, and the elements will melt with fervent heat; both the earth and the works that are in it will be burned up. Therefore, since all these things will be dissolved, what manner of persons ought you to be in holy conduct and godliness, looking for and hastening the coming of the day of God, because of

which the heavens will be dissolved being on fire, and the elements
will melt with fervent heat? (*II Peter* 3:10-12 [NKJV].)

From the earliest hints in *Genesis*, to the scenarios of *II Peter* and
Revelation, there is in the canon of Christian scripture a tendency to more and
more explicit speculation about the last things. In these last sections of
Scripture we find the apostles venturing into picturesque premonitions of the
circumstances of the end times, many of them startlingly like those that figure in
our scientifically-informed, late Twentieth Century imaginings. What (Who?)
put it into a First Century A.D. mind that these possibilities existed in the
natural order: that the *elements* were open to the possibility of melting with
fervent heat; that everything in the world could dissolve, burn up; or that the
heavens could pass away with a great noise? We "know" all this today. We
have been teaching it in the physics books, but only since the end of World
War II.

It seems to me best to understand Peter's words as insights of an
unprecedentedly specific and vivid character, deriving from his privileged
closeness to the mind of Christ, while also (in no contradiction) reflecting the
tendency of all Biblical prophecy. In fact (setting aside for the moment the
peculiar claims of Judaeo-Christian faith, and speaking now generally about the
sources of all faith and cult), *the religious mind* knows about the inevitability
of the end of all things in fire because it knows, *as a moral premise,* that chaos
precedes order. We have no right to expect the life-sustaining structures to
be there, superimposed upon chaos. And (given that they are there) we have no
right to expect them to continue through the next instant. Religion began with,
and is still primarily preoccupied with, beseeching, cajoling, enticing, harassing,
and bribing the Power or Powers behind this cosmos out of withdrawing that
active, benign involvement which overrules the chaos which is previous to the
order.

Philosophers of the past always started from the opposite premise: namely, the givenness of order. This premise appeals to philosophers because it allows us to avoid taking chaos at its full meaning. But the ancient Hebrews agreed with the pagan mind about the primacy (in both a moral and a philosophical sense) of chaos over order. At the same time they did claim to have been shown something in addition to and apart from this general religious knowledge. Against the fact of the tendency to chaos in all the realms of this world of time, the Jews had been given an understanding of God's plan of redemption, the weft of the whole pattern of life, whereby God is in every moment actively, immediately, cancelling out chaos in favour of order.

This knowledge is given to the Jews *in their History*. At the same time, it is *a knowledge about History*. The apostle Peter makes the connections in the letter from which we have already quoted:

> [S]coffers will come in the last days, walking according to their own lusts, and saying, "Where is the promise of His coming? For since the fathers fell asleep, all things continue as they were from the beginning of creation." For this they willingly forget: that by the word of God the heavens were of old, and the earth standing out of water and in the water, by which the world that then existed perished, being flooded with water. But the heavens and the earth which now exist are kept in store by the same word, reserved for fire until the day of judgement and perdition of ungodly men. But, beloved, do not forget this one thing, that with the Lord one day is as a thousand years, and a thousand years as one day. The Lord is not slack concerning His promise, as some count slackness, but is long-suffering toward us, not willing that any should perish but that all should come to repentance (*II Peter* 3:3-9 [NKJV]).

Then follows the passage (10-13), already cited, regarding the last things.

Peter is here responding to his correspondents' appeal for hope in the face of the tendency of all that is real towards chaos. His response is to point *to History*. The Bible tells us that we are being remade for life in a eternal reality by God's direction in the realm of this life. The intimation of our need to be remade in order to be really human; and the related intimation that to be really human is to have an eternal life, is *originally human*: that is, it traces to an original ("Edenic") time when we (Adam) were (was) without knowledge of death; for death, if not contradicted, frustrates all efforts to find meaning in reality. Biblical man does not take for granted the existence of the cosmos, nor the existence of the least thing in it. He does not regard "non-being" as a non-problem. It is not unthinkable to him that all being could give way to non-being. Biblical man understands that the existence of everything and all things requires the constant sustaining action of the original Creator of all. It is because God is constantly active, that anything *is*.

There are evidences of purpose in nature; and if we put our minds to it, we can uncover laws that undergird this purposive behaviour. The Bible, and in particular the *Psalms* and Wisom literature, speak of the pious wonder we should feel as we trace "the ways of God" in our natural environment. But the Bible consistently points out that the sum-total of all the laws that operate in nature is not a true testimony to God, because the will of God is engaged in transforming nature. The laws that ostensibly describe the order of the cosmos actually describe a *tentative system* of order, one which in fact is winding down, and (according to Peter) will end in fire - or in a different visionary metaphor, will be rolled-up like a garment or a scroll. [71]

The Green Tree and the Dry

As Jesus was being led away to crucifixion, "there followed him a great multitude of people, and of women who bewailed and lamented him. But Jesus turning unto them said, 'Daughters of Jerusalem, do not weep for me, but weep for yourselves and for your children, For behold, the days are coming when they shall say, "Blessed are the barren, and the wombs that never bare, and the breasts that never gave suck. Then shall they begin to say to the mountains, Fall on us; and to the hills, Cover us." For if they do these things in a green tree, what shall be done in the dry?' " (*Luke* 23:27-31 [KJV.]

The events of this day of Jesus' trial and execution belong to the time of a green tree. As the tree is green in an early stage of its life, so these events belong to an early time or season (*kairos*) in the progress of the sacred history. People refrain from violence to a tree so long as they prize it, so long as they see advantage or benefit to themselves in letting it remain alive. It would be unnatural to be cutting down and burning green trees. So it is unnatural for the authorities and the acquiescing crowd to be putting Jesus to death in this hour.

He is, thus, speaking of His work, which is to accomplish the sacred history. And He tells us that this work is to be completed over a long period of time. There was an earlier occasion when He told us, speaking from the perspective of eternity, where the whole content of time is known, that Satan had fallen. (*Lk* 10:18) But here He locates Himself in the perspective of this moment in time, and gives us His parting word on the whole course of time to come.

In these parting words we are meant to hear echoes of the themes that figured in His teaching about the course of time to come, delivered more deliberately over the previous week. Again there is reference to trees; and so we must remind ourselves of all the themes associated with these previous words about trees, notably, the words about the fig-trees, discussed in Chapter Three. Again, there is His implicit appeal to our everyday familiarity with nature, and the common wisdom based on this familiarity. We have to be struck, however, by the contrast of occasions and settings. The words we are considering here were not declaimed in a strong voice. The audience is not seated in orderly and respectful silence at the feet of the teacher. There is nothing authoritative in His posture or appearance in this setting. He has endured several hours of spiritual and physical agony of His trial and scourging. He is in the most humiliating of conceivable postures. He is an accused criminal, stripped of His clothing, covered in bloody wounds; He presents an appearance which normally would elicit only disgust. Even if His state of mind and body and spirit were not like this, there would still be no time to develop His themes. He cannot patiently illustrate the meanings of His words with allusions to the History of Israel and the Words of the Prophets, nor with parables. His meaning must be directly intelligible, yet so compacted with allusions to all His previous teaching, and with common wisdom, and with allusions to history and nature, that it serve His hearers (those present and ourselves) until the end of time.

Again , Jesus confirms the wisdom of expecting nature to remain constant and predictable. Our confidence in nature's predictability is well founded in the truth of God's constant rule of nature and of our own lives. But this truth now takes on an utterly new dimension when uttered in this moment of time by this Person. This is the moment of time to which the whole History of the Jews is directed. It is the moment of their judgement. And because the Jews, the people of the Covenant, are the instrument by which God is accomplishing His Plan for the whole of World History, the Plan of Redemption, this moment is the moment which reveals how that History and that Covenant will henceforth come to incorporate the whole of the History of Mankind.

Speaking to the crowd of women, he tells them what they must know, and what their children must know, about the course of events in time, of the history to come. He directs them to nature. He has already taught them that, as they watch "the heavens" for signs, to know how to prepare for tomorrow's weather, so they should watch "the signs of the times." He directs us to nature, because we all have a certain amount of understanding about its course, based upon regular observation, and certain patterns of intelligent response to its course. In the light of all this understanding, it is for our good to acknowledge that there is both natural and unnatural human behaviour. Reasoning from our knowledge of human nature, we see that the reaction of the people to Jesus that day was "unnatural": it was like cutting down green trees. It was violent behaviour, a willful violence against their own interest. And the message to this generation, and generations to come, is that if *"they"* do this now, *"they"* will do as much and worse as time passes, as what is now *"green tree"* becomes *"dry."* No doubt He is thinking of the terrible things that would be literally and actually suffered by many of those standing there that day, and by all their children, of the appalling events of the siege of Jerusalem, described by Josephus. But held at infinite distance from the plane of this life-in-time, it is a conclusive prophecy of the whole course of the history to follow. And as such it tells us conclusively something about the character of all the historical time to follow, something which we must seize, and never let go of, no matter how tempted we may be to go under the authority of other kinds of understanding about what history may contain.

To be reminded in this moment of time about the fact of the constancy of Nature amounts to being told authoritatively that the events of this day do not change the well-understood character of Nature. Neither did His resurrection, nor His ascension, nor the fact that He now sits at the right hand of the God. Neither did any of the events of subsequent History: the destruction of the Temple of the Old Covenant, nor the subsequent scattering and humiliation of the Jews, nor their restoration to Israel. An indeterminate span of time remains before the End, during which the well-understood character of Nature will not change.

But if the well-understood character of Nature is not to change, what will change? The pious mind naturally (so to speak) leaps to another hope: that what happened that day will change *human character*. Indeed, in the remainder of the New Testament scripture we do find many texts that speak of a new nature which is ours in Jesus Christ. The apostles expect and indeed demand unlimited possibilities of reform or character under the effects of their preaching of the gospel. Take this together with the prediction found in *Matthew* 24:14 ("This gospel of the kingdom will be preached throughout the whole world, as a testimony to all nations; and then the end will come"), and we have the foundation for an apparently irresistible expectation: the ensuing centuries will bring about a global change of human character. There have always been pious people whose Theory of History amounts to this. In technical terms, it is the postmillennial understanding of the History of the Church.

But this teaching of Jesus about green and dry trees, and what is natural and unnatural human behaviour, does not sustain such an understanding of the subsequently unfolding of History. It is clear that the apostles believed that evil consequences could not follow from Christian faith. If the tree was good, then the fruit of the tree had to be good. And so we say with them that the effects of Christian faith over the course of world History have been altogether for good. We say that where evil effects adhere to the profession of Christian faith, that the profession was to that degree false; that it follows from our resistance to the changes demanded by that very profession. All *profession* of the gospel is to some degree false. But allowing for this, we insist that the historical effects of Christian faith have been altogether for good.

But it is one thing to claim that the effects of Christian faith have been altogether and everywhere for good and quite another thing to say that the global and total effect of the professional of Christian faith will be to change the character of mankind.

A Hopeful Philosophy of History.

We cannot understand, let alone appropriate for ourselves, the gospel of Jesus Christ without understanding Christ's teaching about World History. This is not to say that Jesus' teaching about History is "more important" than His message about my individual life. It is rather to say that His message about my individual life cannot be separated from His message about History. His message about history is His message about my individual life.

Jesus teaches that my salvation has been accomplished in and through a process that involves and fulfills the whole human story.

Jesus Christ, from His unique perspective of knowledge of the whole content of time, teaches us how to read the record of the past, and what to expect of the future. And He teaches us how to use this understanding to live in hope in the present. If we take with full seriousness the claim that the Church makes about His identity and authority, we must accept and embrace the uniqueness of His knowledge and perspective. It follows that the premises of His teaching about History have conclusive authority. What He offers us is not interesting insights, but absolutely authoritative and conclusive disclosure of all we need to know about the character of reality. And so we must be prepared to let our Theory of History be controlled by this disclosure. And if this disclosure appears at any point to be in conflict with what our mind or anyone else's mind thinks it knows about the character of human History, then there can be no doubt where our allegiance must go.

The very possibility of World History - telling the whole story of mankind as a single story, with linear direction and accumulating meanings - is the unique gift of Christianity to the world. Our Civilization was founded on the Church's understanding that all of humanity was being brought within one destiny by the effects of the message of Jesus Christ regarding How It All Ends. Confidence in the purposefulness of World History was originally sustained by our theologians' understanding that we had been deliberately given some knowledge from the First Show - knowledge from the perspective of eternity, from where it is known How It All Ends. This knowledge is sufficient to assure us that while the processes of Nature will remain unchanged until the end of time, and while human character will remain unchanged until the end of time, nonetheless there is being accomplished in all the detail of World History, and as the outcome of World History's only truly dynamic theme, the globalizing of the gospel, all that needs to be accomplished before man can be reconciled to man, and man can be reconciled to nature, and man-and-nature together can be reconciled to God. The paradoxical character of this hope turns on the understanding that what history is accomplishing to the End of Time will not change the *appearance* of man's alienation. In the dry tree, the character of mankind will indeed seem even more unnatural than in the green.

Give that the governing theme in the intellectual history of our civilization for the past three hundred years has been the determination of our learned leadership to get out from under the "heteronomous" authority of the Creed and to find "autonomy," it has inevitably followed that prevailing theory of history is at odds with theory which follows from the premises of Jesus' teaching. What obscures most people's thinking on this matter is the appearance that our mainstream, textbook and general historiography seemed, at least until recently, to be continuing in something like the character of the traditional Christian historiography. To speak in very large terms: the premise that God is accomplishing through the whole human story an ultimate reconciliation of man to man and man to nature and man-and-nature together to God has clearly been read out of the historiography of our age. But is not the same moral effect accomplished, through inertia, so to speak, by the notion of history as a story of Progress? This line of understanding, which figures largely in the work of Christian theorists of history like Herbert Butterfield, but also is much favoured by many secular theorists (notably, E.H. Carr) deserves respect. But the truth is that a hopeful Theory of History cannot be sustained on any other grounds than the ones we have argued here, and which were originally elaborated by faithful Jews and Christians, depending on their confidence that Prophecy had made known to people of faith something about How It All Ends.

The irony is that modern theory of history began in revolt against the pessimism of the Judaeo-Christian view of man. Liberation of mankind, they said, required throwing-off the shackles of fear of the beyond, the baneful notion of original sin, and the cultural narrowness that caused us to prefer our singular way of telling the whole past of mankind when an infinite number of other equally and even more exciting ways of conceiving the story stood ready to be discovered in the heritage of all the other civilizations. The key to all this hopefulness about the directedness of human history was the Enlightenment's faith in human perfectibility, the vision of another shore to which science was now leading perfectible man. The progressive vision was based on an expectation of fundamental alteration of human character, the eradication of the historical effects of previous unreason.

Jesus' teaching categorically rules out this expectation. The hope under which we live is the hope of Redemption, by God's initiative. The progressive-secular theory of history, which inspired the modern mind until recently, was, as Reinhold Niebuhr brilliantly puts it, the vision of History as it own Christ. Until recently, it was mandatory to write the Prefaces of the World History textbooks in a spirit of hopefulness. Until recently, the positive attitude towards the detailed content of history, initially inspired by and founded upon the promises of the Creed, persisted in an inertial way in secular culture, sustaining apparently patient attention to the detailed record of the past. And the confidence that all this detail was held together by the largest conceivable purposes, by the Divine Plan, persisted in secularized disguise as the Creed of Progress. Insofar as history is still read hopefully, whatever the rationale implied, we see the inertial effects of the Judaeo-Christian hope.

The sobering fact is that today this progressive vision has been altogether leeched out of the textbooks. The Prefaces of the World Civilization textbooks no longer speak confidently of *meanings* that appear to be unfolding in the human story, nor even very convincingly of *direction*. The habits of thought that followed from instruction in the themes of the Creed have atrophied. And consequently - to bring us back to the theme of our Prologue - the study of history and historiographical activity are in steady decline.

*   *   *

Scripture begins by telling us about the origins of everything that exists in in present reality, against a background of chaos; and then about the varieties of life and their beginnings; and then about the origins and the early story of man, the earliest chapters of civilization, the origins of various nations and their distribution across the globe. Then, ostensibly, its focus narrows sharply:

> Now the LORD said to Abram, "Go from your country and your kindred and your father's house to the land that I will show you. And I will make of you a great nation, and I will bless you, and make your name great, so that you will be a blessing. I will bless those who bless you, and those who curse you I will curse; and by you all the families of the earth will bless themselves" (*Genesis* 12:1-3

[NEB.])

The key to the mind of the Bible is that the story is not *narrowing* at this point: it is *widening*. What follows is the story of the overcoming of all the processes that, as the previous Chapters of *Genesis* have shown, lead in the realm of life to death. All the processes at work in this cosmos - the sub-molecular, the physical, the moral, the mental - operate laterally, so to speak, repetitively and predictably; and for this reason alone they are susceptible to review by our sciences and philosophies. The story of the seed of Abraham is the story of the process which leads to the overcoming of all of these lateral processes; it operates vertically, bringing newness into the human situation, building purposefully in a causal way, that can be traced in all the detail we need from that moment to this moment, and building beyond this moment to the End of Times. This process is World History.

Philosophy and science more-or-less vividly describe this tentative system of order. There is, however, a superior dynamic at work in the cosmos which is redeeming this otherwise doomed system of order. This dynamic is God's Plan, *accomplished in History*. This ultimate, cosmic "law" is God's covenant with Abraham, which is presently at work redeeming the whole matrix of order. The "laws of physics" are not independently intelligible. They are not independently lawful. They are subsets, by-laws, of that governing Law-of-laws which in every instant overcomes the lawlessness (the chaos) which physics can see. This Law-of- laws is the historical working-out of God's covenant with Abraham. We could not have found our way to this Law-of-laws through disciplined thought, since thought can only deal with the reality in which it finds itself. We could not find this Plan; we would have to be shown it. And it is precisely the Bible's argument that in the detail of the consequences in time of Abraham's response to God's call we find everything that we need to know about this Plan.

ENDNOTES:

CHAPTER ONE: "THIS IS THE UNIVERSAL WAY."

[1] Augustine, *The City of God*. Trans. by Henry Bettenson, and intro. by David Knowles (Harmondsworth: Penguin, 1972), 422-423.
2 L.S. Stavrianos, *The World Since 1500: A Global History*. 4th edn (Englewood Cliffs, : Prentice-Hall, 1982), xviii-xix.
3 Ibid., 3-4.
4 T. W. Wallbank, et. al., *Civilization Past & Present*. 6th edn. (Glenview: Scott, Foresman, 1986), from "Preface," n.p.
5 John A. Garraty, and Peter Gay (eds.), *The Columbia History of the World* (New York: Harper and Row, 1972), xvii-xviii, & 33-49.
6 Stanley Chodorow, et. al., *A History of the World* (New York: Harcourt, Brace, 1986), iii.
7 J. P. McKay, *et. al., A History of Western Society*. 2nd edn. (Boston: Houghton, Mifflin, 1982.)

CHAPTER TWO: THE LEGACY OF ABRAHAM.

[1] *Hebrews* 11:8ff.
2 A. Leo Oppenheim, *Ancient Mesopotamia: Portrait of a Dead Civilization*. Rev'd edn (Chicago: University of Chicago Press, 1974), 7-30.
3 R. K. Harrison, *Introduction to the Old Testament* (Grand Rapids: Eerdmans, 1969), 96, 109.
4 On *Gen.* 17:5, see: Gunther Plaut, (ed.), *The Torah: A Modern Commentary* (New York: Union of American Hebrew Congregations, 1981), 116-119; *Genesis: A New Translation with a Commentary from Talmudic, Midrashic, and Rabbinic Sources*. Trans. and with a commentary by R. Meir Zlotowitz, and with "Overviews" by Nosson Scherman.: Volume II: *Lech Lecha, and Vayeira* [the portions Gen. 12:1 to 22:24], 562-565; E.A. Speiser, (ed.), *Genesis* [vol. 1 of Anchor Bible Series] (Garden City: Doubleday/Anchor, 1964), 127.
5 See the article, "Ur of the Chaldees" (written by D.J. Wiseman), in *New Bible Dictionary* . 2nd edn. (Philadelphia: Westminster, 1972), 90; *cf.*, A. Leo Oppenheim, *Ancient Mesopotamia: Portrait of a Dead Civilization*. Rev'd edn (Chicago: U. of Chicago Press, 1974), 109ff.
6 John Bright, *History of Israel*. 2nd edn.(Philadelphia: Westminster, 1972), 23-24.
7 Immanuel Kant, "Idea For a Universal History with Cosmopolitan Intent"(1784), in Carl J. Friedrich (ed.), *The Philosophy of Kant: Immanuel Kant's Moral and Philosophical Writings* (New York: Modern Library, 1949), 116-131.
8 A selection of "gleanings" from Jewish literature on the meaning of the Nimrod-figure is in Plaut, *Torah*, 78.

9 Ibid., 83-84.

10 Robert Wenke, *Patterns in Prehistory: Humankind's First Three Million Years.* 2nd edn (New York: Oxford U.P., 1984), 6-7.

11 First published in parts, 1918 to 1919, it appeared as a book in 1920, was frequently revised to 1939, then appeared further revised by Raymond Postgate. It has never, so far as I can tell, been out of print. The edition I use is New York: Garden City, 1956.

12 A contemporary dissenter, equally amateur, equally brilliant, to Wells' anthropology and his historical vision, was G.K. Chesterton, who wrote *The Everlasting Man,* 1925 (Garden City, Doubleday/Image, 1955.)

13 William L. Langer, et. al., *Western Civilization* (New York: Harper & Row, 1968), 12-13.

14 Chodorow, *A History of the World,* xvi, & 8-12.

15 Mario Pei, *The Story of* Language. Revd edn (Philadelphia: Lippincott, 1965), 358-370.

16 Two qualified exceptions to this statement (regarding the uniqueness of Hebrew as a language of the Ancient East, surviving into our time) are Syriac (Aramaic) and Coptic ("Egyptian"). The former is still in use in diminishing pockets of population in Syria and Lebanon, estimated to number a few tens of thousands in all. The latter is still in use as a liturgical language within Christian groups of Hamitic race in Egypt, Ethiopia and Sudan. Both groups, Christian minorities within the Muslim world, have lived as marginal, and frequently repressed communities. Neither language is to be compared with Hebrew as a carrier of a whole tradition from the earliest times to the present. See Arnold Toynbee, *A Study of History,* Vol. XII: *Reconsiderations* (London: Oxford U.P., 1961), Chapter XIII: "The Configuration of Syriac History" (393-461, esp. 396-400) and the subsection on "Fossils," 292-300.

17 Toynbee, *Reconsiderations,* 477.

18 Plaut, *Torah,* 94.

19 F. M. A. de Voltaire, *The Philosophy of History,* 1765. Eng. Trans., with a Preface by Thomas Kiernan (New York: Citadel , 1965), 69-70.

20 Voltaire, *Philosophical Dictionary,* 1764. Trans., with an Introduction and Glossary by Peter Gay (New York: Basic Books, 1962), in Two Volumes. The excerpt is from the article, "Abraham", in Vol. I, 58-62.

21 An excellent overview, ending in conservative conclusions, is Harrison, *Introduction to the Old Testament,* Part One: "The Development of Old Testament Study," 1-82. Cf., William Foxwell Albright. *From the Stone Age to Christianity.* 2nd edn (New York: Doubleday/Anchor, 1957), Chapter 1: "New Horizons in History, " 25-81.

22 Bright, *History of Israel,* 69-71.

23 Peter Gay, *The Enlightenment:An Interpretation.* Vol. II: *The Science of Freedom* (New York: Knopf, 1969), 391.

24 *Essai sur les moeurs,* I, 196, as quoted in Gay, *Enlightenment,* II, 391.

25 Voltaire, the article, "On China", in his *Philosophical Dictionary,* I, 166-70.

26 Gay, *Enlightenment,* II, 391-392. (I have reversed the order in parts of this passage.)

27 Georg Wilhelm Friedrich Hegel, *The Philosophy of History.* Trans. by J. Sibree, and with an intro. by Carl J. Friedrich (New York: Dover, 1956).

28. From the "Introduction to the Dover Edition," not paged.

29 Ibid., 103.

30 Ibid., 116ff.

31 The article, "Writing", in Madelaine & J.M. Miller, (eds.), *New Harper's Bible Dictionary*. 8th edn. (New York: Harper & Row, 1973); or the article, "Writing" in *New Bible Dictionary*; William Foxwell Albright, *The Archeology of Palestine*, revd edn. (Harmondsworth: Penguin, 1960), 185-196. .

32 Stavrianos, *World Since 1500*, 3-4.

33 Chaim Potok, *Wanderings* (New York: Fawcett/Crest, 1978), 473-474, 481-483.

34 The article, "Abraham", in *Philosophical Dictionary*, I, 58-62.

35 Voltaire, *Essai sur les moeurs*, cited by Ernst Cassirer, *The Philosophy of the Enlightenment*, 1932. Trans. From the German by F. Koellen & J. Pettegrove (Boston: Beacon Press, 1955), 219.

36 Leon Poliakov, *The Aryan Myth: A History of Racist and Nationalist Ideas in Europe*. Trans. by E. Howard (New York: "Meridian", 1974.)

CHAPTER THREE: WHAT JESUS TAUGHT ABOUT HIMSELF AND ABOUT HISTORY.

1   The other places in John's Gospel where Jesus says that his time [καιρος... Kairos] or hour [*hora*... ὥρα] has not come are: 7:6, 7:8, 7:30 [*hora*] , 8:20 [*hora*.] When He prepares to go to the cross, He says that His hour [*hora*] has come: 12:23; and cf. 12:27, 13:1.

2   See the section, "Jesus, Man for God", in Karl Barth, *Church Dogm*atics , Vol . III (*The Doctrine of Creation*), Part Two (Edinburgh: T. &T. Clark, 1960), 55-71.

3   Oscar Cullmann, *Christ and Time*. Rev'd edn (Philadelphia: Westminster Press, 1964., 70-71.)

4   Our translators alternate arbitrarily between two words, "heaven" and "sky", when rendering the one Greek word, (ουρανος = *ouranos*.) Looking to the sky is not merely a practical gesture, but is also a pious one, as sky (heaven) is a euphemism for God or Providence, among the Jews as among most religious people everywhere, then and now. Jesus is conceding their piety: they know that there are laws in nature and that the Author of these laws is God.

5   *E.g., Jeremiah* 5:17, *Hosea* 2:17, *Joel* 1:7; *Habakkuk* 3:17.

6   Esp., *Mt* 12:3, *Mk* 2:25; *Lk* 6:3.

7   *Lk* 4:25, *Lk* 9:54.

8   Esp., *Jn* 8.

9   *Mt* 12:40-44, & par.

10 *Mt* 24:15; *Mk* 13:14.

11 Three of the disciples were given a glimpse of this, on the occasion which was called "The Transfiguration" (*Mt* 17:1-8.)

12 *NKJV* reads: " I AM", indicating that these translators understand Jesus to be explicitly claiming identity with the Creator-God, whose true name is not to be uttered - and that His hearers understood Him to be uttering the Name (*Hashem*), and identifying Himself with God.

13 "Sheba" is the remotest corner of Arabia, and is probably to be identified with the

southern coast of the peninsula, present-day Yemen. But the Ethiopians claim her, with some plausibility, as a Queen of their Ancient Kingdom, and the Falashas of Ethiopia claim to derive their Jewish faith and practice from her and their "Jewish blood" from her dalliance with Solomon. This is the context for the story in *Acts* 8:26-40 regarding Philip the Ethiopian eunuch. See Dan Ross, *Acts of Faith: A Journey to the Fringes of Jewish Identity* (New York: St. Martin's, 1982), Chap VIII: "Falashas," 143-166.

14 In *I Kings* 4:25, it is said of Solomon's reign: "And Judah   and Israel dwelt in safety, from Dan   to   Beersheba, every man under his vine and his fig tree." (*Cf., II Kings* 18:31, *Joel* 2:22.) Israel herself is identified with the fig tree in *Hosea* 9:10: "Like grapes in the wilderness I found Israel. Like the first fruit on the fig tree, in its first season, I saw your fathers."

15 *Micah* 4:4 says, of the messianic age, that "they shall sit every man under his vine and fig tree, and none shall make them afraid."

16 *Joel* 1:7, 12: "It [an enemy nation] has laid waste my vines and splintered my fig tree ... The vine withers, the fig tree languishes." Cf. *Amos* 4:9; *Habakkuk* 3:17; *Haggai* 2:19; *Jeremiah* 5:17; *Hosea* 2:12.

CHAPTER FOUR: THE SCANDAL OF END TIMES.

1 Hal Lindsey, *The Late, Great Planet Earth*, 1970 (New York: Bantam, 1973.)

2 See George Gallup, jr. and D. Poling, *The Search for America's Faith* (Nashville: Abingdon, 1980).   Summaries of these and other poll findings appear throughout the pages of Robert Wuthnow, *The Restructuring of American Religion* (Princeton: Princeton U.P., 1988.)

3 John Updike, *A Month of Sundays* (Greenwich, Conn.: Fawcett Books, 1974), 245.

4 Ibid., 244-8.

5 Klaus Koch, *The Rediscovery of the Apocalyptic* (Napierville, Ill.: Allenson, 1972,) 13.

6 Kasemann, cited by John J. Collins, *The Apocalyptic Imagination: An Introduction to the Jewish Matrix of Christianity* (New York: Crossroad, 1987), 1.

7 Collins, *Apocalyptic Imagination,* 2.

8 Henry May, *Ideas, Faiths and Feelings: Essays on American Intellectual and Religious History, 1952-1982* (New York: Oxford, U.P., 1983), 172 -177.

9 Ibid., 177

10 C. Gregg Singer, *A Theological Interpretation of American History.* Rev'd edn, (Phillipsburg, N.J.: Presbyterian and Reform Publishing Co., 1981, 167 - 169.

11 Walter Rauschenbusch, *Christianity and the Social Crisis.* Rev'd edn, 1907, with intro. by Robert Cross, New   York: Harper, 1964),   91 & xxiii;   Walter Rauschenbusch, *Christianizing the Social Order* (New York: Macmillan, 1913), 124.

11 The passage quoted is from his "editorial note" to Arthur C. McGiffert, *The Rise of Modern Religious Ideas* (New York: Macmillan, 1915), vii.

13 Rauschenbusch, *Christianizing the Social Order,* 90.

14 Francis Peabody, *Jesus Christ and the Social Question* (New York: Macmillian, 1901), 120ff.

15 Shirley Jackson Case, "The Premillennial Menace," *Biblical World* (July, 1918), as

199

cited in *Eerdman's Handbook to Christianity in America*, Mark A. Noll, *et. al.* (eds.). Grandrapids: Eerdman's, 1983), 180-181.
16   Albert Schweitzer, *The Quest for the Historical Jesus*. For the impact of the arguments of Schweitzer (his first edition was printed in 1906), see W.R. Hutchinson, *The Modernist Impulse in American Protestantism* (Cambridge: Harvard U.P., 1976), 215ff.
17   Walter Rauschenbusch, *A Theology for the Social Gospel* (New York: Macmillan, 1917), 158.
18   Shirley J. Case, *Millennial Hope* (Chicago: Chicago University Press), 233.
19   Frank Manuel, *The Religion of Isaac Newton* (London: Oxford U.P., 1974), esp. Chapter IV: "Prophecy and History";   Peter Gay, op. cit., I, 314-7 & II, 140-50; Margaret C. Jacob, *The Newtonians and the English Revolution* (Ithica: Cornell U.P., 1976), esp. Chap. 3: "The Millennium", 100-42.
20 Manuel, *Religion of Isaac Newton,* 78; Cf. Richard S. Westfall, *Never At Rest: A Biography of Isaac Newton* (Cambridge: Cambridge U.P., 1980), 327-330.
21 Manuel, *Religion of Isaac Newton*, 4.
22 Ibid., 20.
23 Louis Trenchard More, *Isaac Newton* (New York:Dover, 1934), 605ff.
24 Manuel, *Religion of Isaac Newton*, 4.
25 Maynard Keynes, "Newton the Man," in *Royal Society of London, Newton Tercentenary Celebrations* (Cambridge: Royal Society at the University Press, 1947), 27-34.
26 Manuel, *Religion of Isaac Newton*, 10.
27 Cited by Westfall, 320.

CHAPTER FIVE: KNOWLEDGE FROM THE FIRST SHOW.

[1] Joyce G. Baldwin, *Daniel: An Introduction and Commentary* [Tyndale O.T. Commentary Series] (Downers Grove: InterVarsity Press, 1978), 184.
2 *Inter alia: Lk* 13:34-35, 18:31ff.
3 Schweitzer, *Quest of the Historical Jesus.* Schweitzer's "solution" to the "problem" of Jesus' behaviour is outlined, 349-401. A simpler outline is in A. Schweitzer, *Out of My Life and Thought*, 1933 (New York: Mentor, 1953), Chaps 5 and 6.
4 *Jn* 16:28-30.
5 *E.g.*, of Abraham: *Jn* 8:56-8; of Isaiah: *Mt* 15:7-8, *Lk* 4:16-21, *Jn* 12:37-41: of Daniel, *Mt* 24:15 and par.; of Jeremiah: *Mt* 2:17-18, *Mt* 27: 6-10.
6 *Mt* 11:12-14, 17:9-13, *Mk* 9:9-13; *Lk* 1:16-17, 4:25-30;*Lk* 9:28-36, *Jn* 1:19-34. and *cf.*, *Romans* 11:1-7.
[7] Norval Geldenhuys, *Commentary on the Gospel of Luke* [New International Commentary Series], 1951 (Grand Rapids: Eerdmans, 1983), 523-524.
8   Philip Yancey, "Insights on Eternity from a Scientific Point of View," *Christianity Today*, April 6, 1984, 10.
9 There are problems of chronology with respect to reconciling these texts: for which see Albright, *From Stone Age to Christianity*, 242-243; Harrison, *Introduction*

to OT, 167ff & 316ff; Plaut, *Torah*, 462-463.

10 *Cf., Romans* 4 and *Colossians* 2:9-11.

[11] R.K. Harrison examines the academic literature thoroughly in his *Introduction to the OT*, Part Ten, Chapter I: "Prophets in the Old Testament". See also, the Chapters on the individual books of the "major" and "minor" prophets. With respect to the theories of multiple authorship of *Isaiah*, see 764-800. With respect to the authorship and dating of *Daniel*, 1105-1134, and *cf.*, Baldwin, *Daniel*, 38-44.

12 For the outlines of this history, I recommend the Commentary, already cited, by Baldwin, esp. the section, "Questions of History"), 19-29, from the "Introduction;" or, Harrison, *Introduction to the OT*, 1105-1134. For much more detail, see S.A. Cook, et. al. (eds.), *Cambridge Ancient History*, Vol. VII: *The Hellenistic Monarchies and the Rise of Rome* (Cambridge: Cambridge U.P., 1954), Chapter IV: "Ptolemaic Egypt" (109-153) and V: "Syria and the East" (155-195), both written by M. Rostovtseff; and XXII: "The Struggle of Egypt against Syria and Macedon" (699-731), by W.W. Tarn.

13 Usually identified with the Romans, who made their first intrusion into the politics of the area at this point. Antiochus III was defeated in battle in Thracian Cheresonese, at Thermopylae, and at Magnesia, in 191/190 by Roman forces under Lucius Cornelius Scipio ("Asiaticus"). Then in 168, Roman authority, in the person of Popillius Laenas, ordered Antiochus IV out of Egypt. It was this latter humiliation that drove Antiochus to renew his self-esteem by supression of the Jewish religion.

14 Flavius Josephus, *Jewish War*, I:123-156.

[15] Josephus, *Jewish War*, II:1635f ; Eusebius of Caesarea, *The History of the Church*, (written c. 325 A.D.), III, Chaps. 5 to 8.

16 Josephus, Chaps V-VII; Eusebius, Chaps II-IV; Tacitus, *Annals*, XV:30-44.

17 A classic example is Robert Anderson, *The Coming Prince* (London: Hodder and Stoughton, 1909.)

18. Charlesworth describes the latest archeological work on the Temple Mount and the Old City: "The size of the stones used to build the Temple are [sic] described by Josephus as astronomically massive (Ant. 5.224; 15.392). Scholars have tended to reject Josephus's figures as inflated and exaggerated. Archeological discoveries, however, at Herodion, Masada, and especially in Jerusalem, have proved that Herod the Great was one of the most ambitious and successful builders in antiquity." Charlesworth speaks of individual stones weighing up to 415 tons. In light of these discoveries, "The size and majesty of Herod's Temple Mount has surprisingly loomed large before us." James H. Charlesworth, *Jesus Within Judaism: New Light from Exciting Archeological Discoveries* (New York: Doubleday/Anchor, 1988), 118-119.

19 On Jewish teaching regarding the coming of Messiah, and how that relates to the future of the Temple, see Ephraim E. Urbach, *The Sages: The World and Wisdom of the Rabbis of the Talmud* (Cambridge, Mass.: Harvard U.P., 1987), Chapter XVII: "On Redemption", esp. 649-690.; and Alfred Edersheim, *The Life and Times of Jesus the Messiah*, 3rd edn., 1886 (Grand Rapids: Eerdmans, 1971), vol. II, Chapter VI.

20 Edersheim, *Life and Death of Jesus the Messiah*, Vol. II, 433.

21 *Mt* 24:36: "But of that day and hour no one knows, not even the angels of heaven, nor the Son but the father only". *Cf., Mk.* 13:32. Some early manuscripts omit the phrase "nor the Son".

22 Eusebius, V:1-5.

23   G. A. Williamson, "Introduction" to   Josephus, *Jewish War* (Harmondsworth: Penguin, 1977), 8-9.

24   The puzzling interjection, "Let the reader understand," appears in *Matthew* and *Mark*, but not in *Luke*. Manifestly, these are not Jesus' words. He has been asking His hearers to *listen*; He is not speaking to *readers*. If someone is here calling attention to this text (that is, the text of *Matthew* or *Luke*, the thought occurs that it is someone other than the author. Scholars following this logic therefore speak of this as a marginal aside by a later editor or copier of the original, who is perhaps drawing the attention of readers of this later period (later, that is, than the original audience of Jesus that day, and later as well than the day of the author, Matthew or Luke.) This putative "editor" is drawing the attention of this later generation of Christians to some moment of persecution contemporarty to himself , and he is asking out loud whether that event is somehow prefigured in the text. There was, for example, persecution under Domition (in the 90s), the generally-presumed background to *Revelation*. Perhaps it is Hadrian's construction of the Temple of Jupiter on the ashes of the Temple of the God of Israel that is being alluded to.   But another explanation for the interjection, and one that commends itself to conservative scholars, who prefer to minimize the possibility of significant editorializing upon Jesus' words, is that the original author of the text (Matthew or Mark) is referring his own contemporary readers to a source that they are well-familiar with *as readers* and which is clearly alluded to here, and which they are invited to read: namely, *Daniel*.

25   Geldenhuys, *Commentary on* the Gospel of Luke, 527.

26   Josephus, VI:5.

27   Most   commentaries   take   note   here   of   the   severe earthquake   in Phrygia in 61 A.D., and the famous eruption of Vesuvius in 63. According to Josephus, and the Roman historians as well, the fall of Jerusalem was accompanied by frightening "signs" in the heavens.   Josephus, *Jewish War*, VI:31ff ; Tacitus, *Histories*, V:13 .

CHAPTER SIX : THE RESTORATION OF ISRAEL

1   In part, this paragraph paraphrases Abraham J. Heschel, *Israel: An Echo of Eternity* (New York: Farrar, Straus & Giroux, 1969). 183. For date of and significance of the Meneptah stele, see Harrison, *Old Testament History*, 322-325,

2   Paul Johnson, *A History of the Jews* (New York: Harper & Row, 1987), 1-2.

3   Ibid., 519-520.

4   Cited   by Emil Fackenheim, *Encounters   Between   Judaism and Modern Philosophy* (New York: Schocken, 1980), 218.

5   Ibid., 586-587.

6   Ibid., 374 & 519.

7   Ibid., 519.

8   Marcus Finley, *Ancient History: Evidence and Models* (New York: Viking, 1986), 55.

9   This is to be found in Karl Barth, *Church Dogmatics,* Volume II: *The Doctrine of God* (Edinburgh: T. & T. Clark, 1957),   Part Two, chapter VII:"The Election of God". See esp. the subsections, "Israel and the Church" (195-205) and "The Passing and the Coming Man" (259-305.)

10 Barth, *Church Dogmaitcs*, II:Two, 262-263.

11 Heschel, *Israel: An Echo of Eternity*, 49-51.

12 Eberhardt Busch, *Karl Barth: His Life From Letters and Autobiographical Texts.* Trans by J. Bowden (Philadelphia: Fortress Press, 1976), 492-493.

13 In Volume XII (*Reconsiderations*) of his *Study of History* (London: Oxford, 1961), 292-300), Toynbee defends this classification against the angry rebuttals of Jewish historians, with some bitter and frequently innane arguments.

CHAPTER   SEVEN : BEYOND CHAOS: A CALM LOOK AT HOW IT ALL ENDS

1 Bruce Marshall, (ed.), *The Real World: Understanding the Modern World Through the New Geography* (Boston:Houghton Mifflin, 1991), 15.

2   I am not making this up! See *New York Times Magazine*, October 31, 1982, 25ff.

3   Cited from a current textbook, Louis J. Halle, *Out of Chaos* (Boston: Houghton, Mifflin, 1977), 75.

4 *Isaiah* 34:4; *Rev.* 6:14.

A BIBLIOGAPHICAL ESSAY:

Contemporary University Texts in World History: (consulted for the sections "World History" and "The Efficiency of Our Theory of History.")

Robert J. Wenke, *Patterns in Prehistory: Humankind's First Three Million Years*. Second edn. (New York: Oxford University Press, 1984); John A. Garraty & Peter Gay (eds.), *The Columbia History of the World* (New York: Harper & Row, 1972); Stanley Chodorow, *et. al.*, *A History of the World* (New York: Harcourt, Brace, 1986); Peter N. Stearns, *World History: Patterns of Change and Continuity* (New York: Harper & Row, 1987); L.S. Stavrianos, *The World Since 1500: A Global History*. 4th edn. (Englewood Cliffs: Prentice-Hall, 1982); William L. Langer, et. al., *Western Civilization* (New York: Harper & Row, 1968.)

Biblical History:

Yona Aharoni, and M. Avi-Jonah, *The Modern Bible Atlas* (London: Allen & Unwin, 1979;) William F. Albright, *The Archeology of Palestine*, revised edn. (Harmondsworth: Penguin, 1960); William F. Albright, "Judaism, The Ancient Near East, and the Origins of Christianity," in Norman F. Cantor (ed.), *Perspectives on the European Past: Conversations with Historians* (New York: Macmillan, 1971), Part I, 38-62; William F. Albright, "The Biblical Period," in Louis Finkelstein (ed.), *The Jews: Their History, Culture, and Religion*. 4th edn. (New York: Schocken, 1970), Vol. I, pp. 1-71; William Albright, *From the Stone Age to Christianity*. 2nd edn. (New York: Doubleday/Anchor, 1957); Umberto Cassuto, *The Documentary Hypothesis* (Jersualem: Magnes Press/Hebrew University, 1983); Alfred Edersheim, *Bible History: Old Testament* 4 vols, revised. 1890 * ; Gaalyah Cornfeld & D.N. Freedman, *Archeology of the Bible: Book by Book* (New York: Harper & Row, 1976);

R.K. Harrison, *Introduction to the Old Testament* (Grand Rapids: Eerdmans, 1969); R. K. Harrison, *Old Testament Times* (Grand Rapids: Eerdmans, 1970); J.H. Hayes & J.M. Miller, *Israelite and Judaean History* (Philadelphia: Westminster, 1977); Siegfried Horn, "Recent Illumination of the Old Testament", *Christianity Today*, June 21, 1968, 13-7; Shalom M. Paul & W.G. Dever, *Biblical Archeologyy* (Jerusalem: Keter, 1973); Ephraim A. Speiser, *Genesis* [Anchor Bible, vol. 1] (Garden City: Doubleday/Anchor, 1964); Roland de Vaux, *Ancient Israel: Its Life and Institutions* 2nd. edn. (London: Darton, Longman & Todd, 1965); Walter Vogels, *God's Universal Covenant: A Biblical Study.* 2nd edn. (Ottawa: University of Ottawa Press, 1986.)

A Selection of Biblical Commentaries:

Contemporary Christian Commentaries in multi-volumes:

The Anchor Bible. Edited by William F. Albright & David N. Freedman (Garden City, N.Y.: Doubleday); *New Century Bible Commentaries.* Edited by Ronald Clements & Matthew Black (Grand Rapids: Eerdmans); *New International Commentary on the Old Testament.* Edited by F.F. Bruce (Grand Rapids: Eerdmans); *New International Commentary on the New Testament.* Edited by F.F. Bruce; *Word Biblical Commentary.* Edited by David A. Hubbbard, *et. al* (Word Books: Waco Texas); Robert J. Jamieson, *et. al., Commentary: Practical and Expository on the Whole Bible* (Grand Rapids: Zondervan, 1961); James L. Mays, *et al* (eds.), *Harper's Bible Commentary* (New York: Harper, 1988); Donald Guthrie, *et. al., New Bible Commentary: Revised* (Grand Rapids: Eerdmans, 1970.)

Jewish Commentaries:

A commentary from a liberal Jewish viewpoint, but generously supported from a wide range of Jewish and some Christian and Moslem sources, is

Gunther Plaut (ed.), *The Torah: A Modern Commentary* (New York: Union of American Hebrew Congregations, 1981). A classical Nineteenth-century "neo-Orthodox" commentary is Samson Raphael Hirsch, *The Pentateuch.* (trans. from German by Gertrude Hirschler, edited by Ephraim Oratz (New York: Judaica Press, 1990). A contemporary commentary from an Orthodox viewpoint, is the "Artscroll" Tanach series of Commentaries. From these last I have consulted, *Genesis: A New Translation with a Commentary from Talmudic, Midrashic, and Rabbinic Sources.* Trans. & with a commentary by R. Meir Zlotowitz, and with "Overviews" by Nosson Scherman.

Bible Dictionaries and Word-books:
Anchor Bible Dictionary. 6 vols. Edited by David N. Freedman (Garden City: Doubleday); *New Bible Dctionary.* Second edn.,. (Leicester/Weaton, Ill.:InterVarsity Press, 1982); *New Harper's Bible Dictionary.* 8th edn., edited by Madelaine & J.M. Miller (New York: Harper & Row, 1973); *New Unger's Bible Dictionary* . Edited by R.K. Harrison (Chicago: Moody); *Vine's Expository Dictionary of Old and New Testament Words.* Edited by W. E. Vine, M. F. Unger, *et. al.,* (Old Tappan, N.J.: Fleming Revell, 1981) J.D. Douglas, *et. al.,* (eds), *New Bible Dictionary.* Second edn. (Leicester/Wheaton: InterVarsity/Tyndale, 1962.) Orville J. Nave, *Nave's Concise Topical Bible.*

Philosophy of History in the Age of the Enlightenment:
Karl Barth, *From Rousseau to Ritschl* [the English translation of eleven chapters of *Die Protestantische Theologie im 19. Jahrhundert*] (London: S.C.M. Press, 1959); Peter Gay, *The Enlightenment: An Interpretation.* Vol. I: *The Rise of Modern Paganism* (1966), Vol. II: *The Science of Freedom* (1969) (New York: A.A. Knopf); R.G. Collingwood, *The Idea of History,* edited by T.M. Knox, 1946 (New York: Oxford University Press "Galaxy" ed'n, 1956); Pieter

Geyl, *Debates with Historians* (New York: Meridian Books, 1958); Paul Hazard, *La crise de la conscience Europeene, 1680-1715* (Paris: Editions contemporaines, 1935); Ernst Cassirer, *The Philosophy of the Enlightenment,* 932. Trans. from the German by F. Koelln & J. Pettegrove (Boston: Beacon Press, 1955); F.M.A. de Voltaire, *The Philosophy of History.* 1765. Eng. trans., with a Preface by Thomas Kiernan (New York: Citadel, 1965.)

Nineteenth-Century Philosophy of History.

Carl J. Friedrich (ed.), *The Philosophy of Kant: Immanuel Kant's Moral and Political Writings* (New York: Modern Library, 1949); George Peabody Gooch, *History and Historians in the Nineteenth Century.* Revised edn. (Boston: Beacon, 1959); G. W.F. Hegel, *The Philosophy of History.* 1823. Trans. by J. Sibree. Intro. by C.J. Friedrich) New York: Dover, 1956); J. G. von Herder, *Reflections on the Philosophy of the History of Mankind.* Abridged, and with an introduction by Frank E. Manuel (Chicago: University of Chicago Press, 1968.)

Contemporary Studies and Commentaries on Meaning in History :

Herbert Butterfield, *Man On His Past:The Study of the History of Historical Scholarship* (Cambridge: Cambridge University Press, 1969); Herbert Butterfield, *The Origins of History* (New York: Basic Publishers, 1981); R.G. Collingwood, *The Idea of History* (New York: Oxford University Press/Galaxy, 1956); M.C. D'Arcy, *The Meaning and Matter of History: A Christian View* (New York: Farrer, Strauss, & Giroux, 1957); George Peabody Gooch, *History and Historians in the Nineteenth Century* (Boston: Beacon, 1959); Van A. Harvey, *The Historian and the Believer* (New York: Macmillan, 1966); E. Harris Harbison, *Christianity and History* (Princeton: Princeton University Press, 1964); Arthur O. Lovejoy, *Essays in the Idea of History* (Baltimore: John Hopkins

University Press, 1948); Karl Lowith, *Meaning in History*, 1949 (Chicago: U. of Chicago Press "Phoenix" ed'n, 1957); C. T. McIntire, (ed.), *God, History, and Historians: An Anthology of Modern Christian Views of History* (New York: Oxford University Press, 1977); C.T. McIntire, (ed.), *Herbert Butterfield: Writings on Christianity and History* (New York: Oxford University Press, 1979); John Warwick Montgomery, *The Shape of the Past: A Christian Response to Secular Philosophies of History* (Minneapolis: Bethany Fellowship Press, 1975); John Warwick Montgomery, *History and Christianity* (Downers Grove, Illinois: InterVarsity, 1965); John Warwick Montgomery, *Where Is History Going? A Christian Response to Secular Philosophies of History* (Minneapolis: Bethany Fellowship, 1969); C. A. Patrides, *The Grand Design of God: The Literary Form of the Christian View of History* (Toronto: University of Toronto Press, 1972); Eric C. Rust, *Towards a Theological Understanding of History* (New York: Oxford University Press,1963.)

Sources for the historical context of Jesus' eschatological teaching (as discussed in Chapter Three.)

(I) Historical Context for the Prophecies of Daniel:
Out of the host of commentaries on the Book of *Daniel*, I recommend Joyce G. Baldwin, *Daniel: An Introduction and Commentary* [Tyndale O.T. Commentary Series] (Downers Grove: InterVarsity, 1978.) On the historical context, see the section, "Questions of History" (pp. 19-29) from the "Introduction." Also: Harrison, *Introduction to the OT*, pp. 1105-34. For the details of the history, see: S.A.Cook, et. al., eds.), *The Cambridge Ancient History*. Vol. VII: *The Hellenistic Monarchies and the Rise of Rome* (Cambridge University Press, 1954), Chap. IV: "Ptolemaic Egypt" (pp. 109-153), and Chap. V: "Syria and the East" (155-195), both written by M. Rostovtseff; and Chap. XXII: "The

Struggle of Egypt against Syria and Macedon" (pp. 699-731), by W.W. Tarn.

(ii) Historical Context for Jesus' Eschatological Teaching and its Reception by the Early Church:

(a) Primary sources:

For the forty years between the Resurrection and the fall of the Second Temple, there is an extraordinary quantity of historical documentation, by the standards of Ancient History, and even by the standards of Roman History. (To get some notion of what these standards are, consult Marcus I. Finley, *Ancient History: Evidence and Models* (New York: Viking, 1986), Chaps 2 ["The Ancient Historian and His Sources"] and 3 ["Documents".] The most detailed source for the events of the period is the historian, Flavius Josephus (born 37/38 A.D., died sometime after 94/95), who was a member of a leading Jewish family, and a leader in the early months of the insurrection, but who defected, and became in effect the self-appointed justifier of the Roman victory, going in fact to the extreme point of having himself adopted into the family of the conqueror, Titus Flavius Vespasianus, and taking their name. Later, he sought to reclaim his Jewish identity through works which glorified the Jewish past (his *Antiquities of the Jews* (c. 93-94.) For his *Jewish War* (written c. 74-79) I use the trans. by G.A. Williamson, revised, 1970 (Harmondsworth: Penguin, 1977). On the Roman side, there are two works by Tacitus (c. 55-c.117): *The Histories* (publ'd c. 109), covering the period from his own youth down to the death of Domitian; and *The Annals* (c.117), covering the prior period beginning with Tiberius (r.14-37), down to the 60's (although the last sections have not survived intact). For *The Histories*, I use the trans. by Kenneth Wellesley (Harmondsworth: Penguin, 1972). For the matter of Rome's dealings with Judaea, c. 30 A.D. and thereafter) see esp. II:4, II:74-81, V:1-13. For *The Annals*, I use the trans. by Michael Grant, revised 1977

(Harmondsworth: Penguin, 1977). The other principal contemporary Roman source is Suetonius (c. 69-c.140), *The Twelve Caesars* (publ'd c. 120). I use the trans. by Robert Graves (Harmondsworth: Penguin, 1957). For the matter of Rome's dealings with Judaea, c. 30 A.D. and after) , see X-XI . A convenient sampler of all this literature is in Barrett (see below.)

For many centuries, the Church used as its "textbook" on the subject of its early history Eusebius of Caesarea, *The History of the Church*, which was published somewhere around 325 A.D. It is based on the recollections handed down within the Church and upon earlier works of Church history, many of which are copied out at length. I use the Penguin edition, translated by G.A. Williamson (Harmondsworth: Penguin, 1965).

(b) Modern scholarly commentaries on this Early History of the Church :

C. K. Barrett, (ed.), *The New Testament Background: Selected Documents* (New York: Harper & Row, 1961); Pierre Benoit, *Jesus and the Gospel*. Vol. I (London: Darton, Longman, & Todd, 1973); F.F. Bruce, *New Testament History* (Garden City: Doubleday/Anchor, 1972); James H. Charlesworth, *Jesus Within Judaism: New Light from Exciting Archeological Discoveries* (New York: Doubleday/Anchor, 1988); Haim Cohn, *The Trial and Death of Jesus* (New York: Ktav, 1977); Alfred Edersheim, *The Life and Times of Jesus the Messiah*, 3rd edn., 1886 (Grand Rapids: Eerdmans, 1971); David Flusser, *Jesus*. 2nd edn. (Jerusalem: Hebrew University, 1998); Michael Green, *Evangelism in the Early Church* (London: Hodder & Stoughton, 1970); Paul Johnson, *A History of Christianity* (Harmondsworth: Penguin, 1980); Joseph Klausner, *Jesus of Nazareth: His Life, Times, and Teaching* , 1922. Trans. from the Hebrew by H. Danby (New York: Menorah Publishing, 1925); John P. Meier, *A Marginal Jew: Rethinking the Historical Jesus* , Vol I (New York: Doubleday, 1991); Harold D. Hoehner, *Herod Antipas: A Contemporary of Jesus Christ* (Grand Rapids:

Zondervan, 1980); Everett F. Harrison, *Introduction to the New Testament* . Revised edn. (Grand Rapids: Eerdmans, 1982); George Foot Moore, *Judaism In the First Centuries of the Christian Era: The Age of Tannaim.* 1927. (Peabody, Mass.: Hendrickson, 1997.)

Scholarly Studies in the Field of Modern Biblical Criticism:

An excellent brief summary of the literature is in the Anchor Bible Commentary series, the volume by W.F. Albright & Mann, *Matthew* (Garden City: Doubleday/Anchor, 1971), pp. xix-cxcviii. Fuller surveys are: John Dillenberger & Claude Welch, *Protestant Christianity: Interpreted Through Its Development* (New York : Scribner's, 1958); Gerhard Maier, *The End of the Historical-Critical Method* .Trans. by E.W. Levernz & R.F. Norden (St. Louis: Concordia, 1977); James Samuel Preus, *From Shadow To Promise: Old Testament Interpreteation from Augustine to Young Luther* (Cambridge, Mass.: Harvard U.P., 1969); Albert Schweitzer, *The Quest of the Historical Jesus: A Critical Study of Its Progress From Reimarus to Wrede.* 3rd edn. (London: A. & C. Black, 1956) ; Claude Welch, *Protestant Thought in the Nineteenth Century* . Vol I: 1799:1870 (New Haven: Yale Univesity Press, 1972.)

Eschatology:

The Jewish Tradition:

G. F. Moore, *Judaism,* Part VII: "The Hereafter" (II: 279-395); D. S. Russell, *The Method and Message of Jewish Apocalyptic* (Philadelphia: Westminster, 1964); D. S. Russell, *the Method and Message of Jewish Apocalyptic* ((Philadelphia: Westminster, 1964.)

In the Seventeenth and Eighteen Centuries:

Frank Manuel, *The Religion of Isaac Newton* (London: Oxford U.P., 1974), esp. Chapter IV: "Prophecy and History"; Peter Gay, *The Enlightenment*, I: 314-317, & II: 140-50; Margaret C. Jacob, *The Newtonians and the English Revolution* (Ithica: Cornell University Press, 1976), esp. Chap. 3: "The Millennium.", pp. 100-142; Richard S. Westfall, *Never At Rest: A Biography of Isaac Newton* (Cambridge: Cambridge University Press, 1980); Derek Gjertsen, *The Newton Handbook* (London: Routledge & Kegan Paul, 1986), esp. "Interpretations and purposes of prophecy" (pp. 273-275), and "Observations upon the Prophecies of Daniel and the Apocalypse of St. John" (pp. 396-399). The last English edition of the "Observations" is that of William Whittla, London, 1922. Louis Trenchard More, *Isaac Newton* (New York: Dover, 1934.) The fullest treatment of Newton's religious writing is in the book by Manuel, where we find an "Appendix A", containing fragments of Newton's treatise on Revelation, and Appendix B, a fragment of the "Synchronisms," Newton's essay on Biblical chronology related to the record of ancient history.

Contemporary Christian Eschatology.

Robert Anderson, *The Coming Prince* (London: Hodder and Stoughton, 1909); Artur E. Bloomfield, *The End of the Days: The Prophecies of Daniel Explained* (Minneapolis: Bethany Fellowship, 1961); Charles L. Feinberg, *Millennialism: The Two Major Views.* 3rd & enlarged edn. (Chicago: Moody, 1980); Harold Lindsell, *The Gathering Storm: World Events and the Return of Christ* (Wheaton: Tyndale, 1981); Hal Lindsey, *The Late, Great Planet Earth,* 1970 (New York: Bantam, 1973); J. Dwight Pentecost, *Things to Come: A Study in Biblical Eschatology,* 1958 (Grand Rapids: Zondervan, 1964).

Contemporary Scholarly Studies:

John J. Collins, *The Apocalyptic Imagination: An Introduction to the Jewish Matrix of Christianity* (New York: Crossroad, 1987); Klaus Koch, *The Rediscovery of the Apocalyptic* . Trans. from German (Napierville, Ill.: Allenson, 1970.)

The Politics of Kingom theology

Social Gospel:

Robert T. Handy, (ed.), *The Social Gospel in America: Gladden, Ely, Rauschenbusch* (New York: Oxford University Press, 1966); Richard Hofstadter, (ed.), *The Progressive Movement 1900-1915* (Englewood Cliffs: Prentice-Hall, 1963); Charles Hopkins, in *The Rise of the Social Gospel in American Protestantism, 1865-1915* (New Haven: Yale University Press, 1940); W.R. Hutchinson, *The Modernist Impulse in American Protestantism* (Cambridge: Harvard U.P., 1976); Henry May, *Ideas, Faiths and Feelings: Essays on American Intellectual and Religious History, 1952-1982* (New York: Oxford, University Press, 1983); Arthur C. McGiffert, *The Rise of Modern Religious Ideas* (New York: Macmillan, 1915); Walter Rauschenbusch, *Christianity and the Social Crisis* . 1907. (Revised edn. with intro. by Robert Cross , New York: Harper, 1964); Walter Rauschenbusch, *Christianizing the Social Order* (New York: Macmillan, 1913); C. Gregg Singer, *A Theological Interpretation of American History* Revised edn. (Philadelphia: Presbyterian & Reformed, 1981;); James Turner, *Without God: Without Creed: The Origins of Unbelief in America* (Baltimore: Johns Hopkins, 1985); Willem A. Visser't Hooft, *The Background of the Social Gospel in America* . 1928. (Reprinted edn., n.d., St. Louis: Bethany Press.)

Contemporary Premillennialism:

Paul Boyer, *When Time Shall Be No More: Prophecy Belief in Modern American Culture* (Cambridge, Mass.: Harvard University Press, 1992); Timothy P. Weber, *Living in the Shadow of the Second Coming* (enlarged ed., Grand Rapids: Zondervan/Academie, 1978); Ernest R. Sandeen, *The Roots of Fundamentalism: British and American Millenarianisms, 1800-1930*, 1970. (Reprinted. Grand Rapids: Eerdmans, 1978.)

Liberal Critique of Premillennial Literature:

Shirley Jackson Case, "The Premillenial Menace," in *Biblical World*. 1918; Shirley Jackson Case, *The Millennial Hope: A Phase of Wartime Thinking* (Chicago: University of Chicago Press, 1918); Frances J. McConnell, "The Causes of Premillenarianism", *Harvard Theological Review* XII (April, 1919), 179-92; Rauschenbusch, *A Theology for the Social Gospel*, Chap. 18: "Eschatology," 208-239.

....

TORONTO STUDIES IN THEOLOGY